Intentional diversity

Intentional diversity

Creating Cross-Cultural
Ministry Relationships in Your Church

BY
JIM LO

wesleyan
publishing
house

Indianapolis, Indiana

Copyright © 2002 by Wesleyan Publishing House
Published by Wesleyan Publishing House
Indianapolis, Indiana 46250
Printed in the United States of America
ISBN-13: 978-0-89827-242-0
ISBN-10: 0-89827-242-4

The Color of God

What color is God?
Asked the child with skin so fair.
Is He white like me?
Does He have light hair?

Is God dark like me?
Asked the child with skin of golden hue.
Has He hair that's dark and curly?
Are His eyes brown or blue?

I think God is red like me,
The Indian boy is heard to say.
He wears a crown of feathers,
And turns our nights to day.

Each of us knows that God is there,
In all the colors above.
The one color He truly is,
Is the beautiful color of Love.

So when your soul goes to heaven,
When your life comes to an end,
He will be waiting, and His hand to you
Will He extend.

There will be no colors in Heaven,
What counts isn't different or same,
You will be judged by your earthly deeds,
Not your color or your name.

So when your time comes,
And you see God in His heaven above,
Then you will see the only color that counts—
The Brilliant Color of Love.

—Rachel Leep

Contents

Introduction

*The biggest thing I do not like about New York are the foreigners. I'm
not a very big fan of foreigners. You can walk an entire block in Times
Square and not hear anybody speaking English. Asians and Koreans and
Vietnamese and Indians and Russians and Spanish people and everything
up there. How . . . did they get here?*

—John Rocker, professional baseball player

On a lazy Saturday afternoon in Zimbabwe, my two sons and I were examining some American coins. Using a magnifying glass—one that Sherlock Holmes would have appreciated, no doubt —we inspected pennies, nickels, dimes, and quarters. The phrase *E Pluribus Unum* appeared on every coin. I chuckled to myself as my six-year-old twins tried to pronounce these "foreign words."

"Dad, what does *EE Plow-REE-bus OO-nom* mean?"

Out of many, one is not an easy concept for young children to grasp. As best I could, I explained the idea that from many people could come one nation.

STRENGTH THROUGH UNITY

In the early history of the United States, Americans strove to create a common identity. Their goal—having come to America from all over the world—was to conform. Downplaying individual differences, they worked to create a society that would meld them into one nation. By so doing, they aimed to achieve strength through unity.

However, this is no longer the goal of many Americans. Approximately twenty years ago, sociologists Nathan Glazer and Patrick Moynihan caused quite a stir when they stated that America had oversold itself as a "melting pot." They found that individuals who had been stirred into the pot simply refused to be "melted." In other words, people living in America now passionately hold on to their ethnic identities. Author Russell Baker echoes this sentiment, stating that, for Americans, the future will be all *Pluribus* and no *Unum!*

DEFINING MAJORITY AND MINORITY GROUPS

When I served as a missionary, I had the opportunity to speak in many different churches. It is my observation that the Church, generally speaking, is not reaching people who are "different." I base my observation on two types of comments I've heard: (1) those from individuals who belong to the "minority group" and (2) those from individuals who belong to the "majority group."

In sociological circles, the term "majority group" refers to any group that is dominant in a society. Stated differently, a majority group is any group that enjoys more than a commensurate portion of the wealth, power, or status in a society.

By contrast, a "minority group" is any group assigned to an inferior status in a society. Those who are part of the minority have a less-than-proportional share of wealth, power, or social status. In many instances, members of the majority group discriminate against members of the minority group. As a rule, a majority group is in a position to dominate or exercise power over minority groups.

It is important to understand two things about majority and minority groups. First, even though membership in either group is frequently based upon race or ethnicity, factors such as gender, physical disability, lifestyle, or sexual orientation may also determine group identification.

Second, whether a group is considered a majority or a minority group does not necessarily correspond to the number of people in the group. A person may belong to a group that comprises a majority of the population yet is considered a minority. An example of this is seen in South Africa, where 80 percent of the population is black. Until recently, Blacks were considered to be the minority group and were forced to exist in a subordinate role to white South Africans.

MINORITY GROUP COMMENTS

Minorities are not always made to feel welcome in churches where they are ethnically different from the majority of the congregation. That's my conclusion based on comments I've heard personally, as well as from the reports of others who have shared their experiences with me. One black pastor was ready to leave his denomination because he had never felt accepted by the pastors in his district, most of whom were white. A man of Hispanic background said this:

> The people of this church try to be nice . . . but their friendliness seems so artificial to me. They have this way of always pointing me out during the worship service . . . almost as if they are saying, "Look at us, we have broken the color lines." It feels uncomfortable. . . . I feel like the token Mexican.

Recently, a Japanese Christian man phoned the university where I teach. He wanted to talk to me because he had heard that I am Chinese and live in a predominantly white region. "Jim, I am considering moving to your state, but I have concerns. How will Christians there treat my family and me? We have had enough negative experiences to make us shy about moving. White Christians have not always treated us kindly."

And it is not always people of color who are different. Caucasians can be the minority group too. Some Whites who have visited African-American churches have told me they were made to feel uncomfortable and out of place. For example, ushers seated one white couple in the front of a church, very near the pulpit. The sermon that Sunday dealt with how the white race had poorly treated the black race throughout history. Every time the pastor referred to Whites in the sermon, the young couple felt as though the eyes of the congregation shifted from the pastor to them. It made them feel "creepy."

MAJORITY GROUP COMMENTS

Invited to speak at a church one Sunday, I arrived early in order to spend time in prayer and preparation for my sermon. The white-painted sanctuary was silent until approximately 9:15 A.M., when people began to trickle in. Because no greeters had arrived, I thought, "Jim, why not be helpful and be the temporary church greeter? You can hand out the bulletins and make the people feel welcome."

The next person to enter the church looked at me with unfriendly, piercing eyes. Without uttering a word, he grabbed the bulletin from my hand and proceeded quickly into the sanctuary. Following him, a woman stared at me questioningly, grunted some incomprehensible words, and went on her way.

Some elderly women now made their way up the stairs and into the sunlit foyer where they were met by the "new greeter." Two of the ladies rudely snatched bulletins from my hand as they went around me to the cloakroom. In a loud whisper, one of the ladies commented, "Who's that? We don't want that kind in our church. Why doesn't he worship with his own kind?"

Perhaps you are wondering what is wrong with me. Do I have some kind of contagious disease or one eye in the center of my forehead?

I believe the people of that church reacted to me negatively because I am an ABC—American-Born Chinese. Because my appearance differs from the majority (depending on where you live), Christian people have often treated me rudely, as if I were stupid, or immune to unkind gestures and remarks.

I can understand when nonbelievers treat me this way. However, I do not understand how Christians— who regularly testify about their salvation experience and sing "I'm so glad I'm a part of the family of God"—can mistreat other Christians because they have a different skin color.

Many minorities, like me, were born in America. Having grown up in America, we "feel" and "think" American. However, when we enter a situation in which we are the minority because of our skin color, hair texture, or eye shape, we are sometimes made to feel as if we were intruders or even dangerous.

A STRUGGLING CHURCH

I was to speak at one church about what God was doing on the mission field. My wife, Roxy, accompanied me. As is our custom, we arrived early to set up our missionary display. Completing this task, I walked over to join my wife, who was talking to an older woman. As I drew near, I overheard part of their conversation. This woman must not have realized that Roxy and I are married. That might have been because Roxy is not Chinese like me (poor girl); she is Caucasian.

Speaking loudly enough for me to hear, the woman said, "I don't know why that Chinese guy has come to our church. If he wants to worship, he should find a Chinese church to attend."

Upon hearing her comments, I realized why her church was struggling. At one time the church had had more than 250 people in attendance. The Sunday morning we gave our presentation, the attendance was around sixty. The reason for the decline was not that the neighborhood was dying. In fact, the population around the church was increasing due to an influx of Asians, African Americans, and Hispanics. The Christians in this church, however, did not *want* people of other races to attend. Their bias was evident in other comments I heard during our time with them:

"If we allow them to come here, they will only dirty up the place."

"They are a bunch of leeches. They wouldn't help us financially. Instead, they would expect us to support them. Don't you know that they are all on welfare?"

"Those kind don't become real Christians. They will always hold on to their old ways even though they say they are Christians. We need to keep the purity of our faith."

THE REASON FOR THIS BOOK

The theme of this book is that God's Kingdom should include everyone; therefore, we must seek to reach everyone.

While promoting cross-cultural church planting, evangelism expert Marlin Mull stated:

Comfort zones restrict and bind many local churches. We feel concern for local church needs, which is legitimate, yet we can easily forget the needs of others. Do the needs of others (including those from different cultural backgrounds) make us uncomfortable enough to forego the current comfort of our church life?[1]

Missions professor David Hesselgrave states that "religious, cultural, social, ethnic, and other barriers must be crossed if the Great Commission is to be obeyed."[2] He further contends that even though the Church in America talks about wanting to reach every person with the message of Christ, it has not gone far enough to make this a reality. The American Church has turned away "from the hard work of seeking to understand other worldviews and relating meaningfully to people who hold them."[3]

Though overseas mission efforts have demonstrated some success in reaching people of different cultural backgrounds, the home evangelistic effort has not been as effective with those who are ethnically different. In obedience to God, the Church in North America must choose acceptance of, and cultural sensitivity to, those from different ethnic backgrounds. If that is to happen, it must begin with individual Christians—like you—who are willing to move out of their comfort zones and intentionally create relationships with people of other cultures.

Chapter One

The World Is Shrinking!

America has the second largest African-American population next to Nigeria, and the largest Polish population next to Poland. New York is the second largest Puerto Rican city. Greater Los Angeles is home to the second largest Hispanic population in the world. . . . Los Angeles has 1.2 million Asians and 4.5 million Hispanics.

—Jerry Appleby, *Missions Have Come Home to America*

When I was eight years old, I attended the New York World's Fair with my family. I was amazed to be among thousands upon thousands of people, all with the same goal of experiencing this remarkable event. As we walked around, we overheard people saying, "You *must* go to the Disney pavilion. Their show is wonderful! It's the best I've seen!" So, guess where I wanted to go!

The line to enter the Disney pavilion was long, but it was worth the wait. Once inside, we were seated in small boats and strapped in. When a boat was filled to capacity, it moved forward, giving the passengers a tour of many different cultures of the world. Dressed in native costumes, animated dolls and animals danced and sang in the languages of many countries. One song was played again and again throughout the ride: *It's a Small World*. All too soon the ride was over. (I wanted it to go on and on.) As we exited the boats, a man behind me said, "That shows how the world is shrinking."

His words hit me like a bolt of lightning and played havoc with my eight-year-old imagination! The world was shrinking? When had that happened? If the world was getting smaller and smaller, would there be enough room left for me when I became a "big person"? For several nights I lost sleep, wrestling with the problem of our shrinking world.

FEAR: A COMMON REACTION

In those days, my brothers, Bill and Tom, and I liked to play King of the Mountain in a park near our home. Slim, strong, and very agile, my brothers excelled at whatever sport they tried. I was short, pudgy, and not very athletic.

As you can guess, I was never the king. Once the signal was given, my brothers would join forces and gang up on me. Their idea was to get rid of the "wimp" first. It did not take much for them to trip me and send me rolling down the hill.

As I lay in bed thinking about the shrinking world, I arrived at this conclusion: If I couldn't even win a game of King of the Mountain with my brothers, I would stand no chance of winning the right to a small spot on a shrinking planet when I finally became a man. My worst fear was being shoved off the globe and left to float aimlessly in space—a nightmarish thought for a young lad! It wasn't until much later that I realized people didn't mean that our planet was physically shrinking when they said the world was growing smaller.

I know what you must be thinking: Jim wasn't very bright, was he? But fear is a very common reaction to the "shrinking" of the planet. Due to a variety of factors, people of different cultures now have more opportunities to come in contact with one another. People of other cultures are no longer far away, even when they live in another country. We live much closer together because many of the obstacles that used to separate us are gone. While this is seen as a positive step by many people, others find it threatening.

E PLURIBUS UNUM

E Pluribus Unum (out of many, one)—the motto on the Great Seal of the United States of America, the same motto my sons found on their coins—is an accurate description of America. My wife, Roxy, is an American of German descent. I am of Asian ancestry, yet I am an American. My friend Ashwil is black, and she is an American. Another friend, Carmela, is Indian, and she is an American. Although Americans are ethnically diverse, our goal is to be unified. We have *many* ethnicities, but we are *one* in that we are all Americans.

In many ways American culture reminds me of the Zambesi River, which flows through Zimbabwe. When I arrived in Africa as a missionary, I assumed that the Zambesi was a single river. An African pastor corrected me. He explained that the Zambesi is made up of many streams and tributaries. In the same way, America comprises many types of people who come from many different backgrounds.

Recently, I drove my sister-in-law Sherry to the airport. She was headed home after visiting us for a week. As we queued up at the check-in line, I decided to see how many different cultural groups I could identify. I saw white Americans, African Americans, Hispanics, Muslims, Chinese, Japanese, Africans, Indians, Native Americans, Spaniards, and Britons. All of these groups were represented at the Indianapolis International Airport. It seems that the airport was appropriately named!

People of color live all around us. The National Center for Education Statistics reports that 30 percent of the students in the United States in 1990 were not Caucasian. In 1994, the number increased to 34 percent. It is predicted that by the year 2010, the number of non-Caucasian students in the United States will be more than 40 percent.

Another report indicates that in San Jose, California, the surname "Nguyen" outnumbers the surname "Jones" in the telephone book. In many toy stores, Barbie dolls are no longer Caucasian only. There are also African-American, Native American, and Hispanic Barbie dolls.

We do not live in isolation. Contact with individuals from other ethnic backgrounds is inevitable.

WHY THE WORLD IS SHRINKING

In their book, *Personality in Nature, Culture and Society*, C. Kluckkohn and H. A. Murray commented: "Every person is, in many respects, like all other people, like some other people, like no other person."[1] As early as 1948, they recognized that our world was getting smaller. Four major factors have contributed to this shrinkage: increased mobility, high-tech communication, changes in the international business community, and politics.

Increased Mobility

A jumbo jet can take us from one part of the world to another in a matter of hours. It fascinates me that I can be in exotic, ancient Cambodia one day and in modern America some thirty hours later. Ease of movement is definitely shrinking our world.

Students from other countries, including exchange students, enter many American high schools, universities, and colleges. Students from Europe, Africa, Asia, and Latin America attend the university where I teach. Businesspeople from overseas come to the States to study business, as well as to market their products. Military personnel from other countries are stationed here for brief periods to learn military strategy. One such couple is Chipo Makusha and her husband. They attended the Kumalo Wesleyan Church in Bulawayo, Zimbabwe. Last year they came to Washington, D.C., so that Chipo's husband could receive military training. His aim is to return to Africa and train others.

Tourists can be found in every major American city. While visiting my brother in Brooklyn, New York, I spotted a group of around fifty Filipinos, all wearing pink T-shirts that read: "We are Filipino tourists going to see the home of Elvis." Now that has to make you smile! More than two million people attended the millennium celebration in Times Square on New Year's Eve 2000. CNN reported that the majority of these people were from other countries. Opportunities for cross-cultural interaction abound as never before, and these opportunities will continue as modes of transportation proliferate.

High-Tech Communication

The development of intricate, innovative, and sophisticated communication systems has also promoted cross-cultural contact. Advances in mail systems, publishing, film production, television, and news services facilitate our contact with people from different parts of the world.

Computers and Electronic Mail. When Roxy and I went to Africa in the early 1980s, it took an average of two weeks for mail to reach us from the States. We thought that was pretty good at the time, especially after an older missionary told us that he could remember when it took up to three months for mail to reach him.

In recent years electronic mail has significantly accelerated the rate at which communications can be delivered to others around the world. This week I have already e-mailed missionary friends in Cambodia, South Africa, Zimbabwe, the Philippines, Honduras, Brazil, and Mongolia. If my timing is right, I can receive a reply within minutes of sending a message. Incredible, if you ask me!

The Film Industry. The film industry is also shrinking our world. Africans of the Chinotimba Township in Victoria Falls, Zimbabwe, regularly gather on Saturday nights at the central market. Their purpose for gathering is to watch American movies shown on a blank billboard that has been painted white. *Forrest Gump*, *Santa Clause*, and *Godzilla* are just a few of their favorites. (It was humorous to hear Tom Hanks speaking Shona.)

While the film industry helps those in other countries learn more about American culture, it also helps Americans learn more about other cultures. American moviegoers have seen films dealing with such subjects as Buddhism (*Little Buddha*), Chinese history, Australian culture (*Crocodile Dundee*), Jewish pain (*Schindler's List*), African tribalism (*Shaka Zulu*), and Cambodian sorrow (*The Killing Fields*). Even as I write, *Anna and the King* is making its debut in theaters across America. Filmed in Asia, this movie uses many Southeast Asian actors and actresses in key roles.

Television. When I was visiting a remote village in Mozambique, the children of the village learned that I was from America. Their most frequently repeated question was, "Do you know Michael Jordan?" I was surprised that these Mozambicans, who were living in mud huts without electricity and running water, knew about Michael Jordan. When I questioned them about this, they replied, "We watch American television." One of the men in the village had purchased a television set and an electric generator. In order to pay for his investment, he charged the other villagers for watching television with him. Reruns of American basketball games were a favorite of these Mozambican viewers.

Television exposes Americans to other cultures also. On any given night, one can tune the television to the Travel Channel or the Discovery Channel and take a visual tour of China, Africa, Indonesia, or the Caribbean Islands. National Geographic programs introduce many Americans to the numerous and diverse cultures of the world. With one push of a remote-control button, I can walk dirt jungle paths to visit the Yanomamo tribe of South America. With another click, I can visualize what it would be like to eat raw fish with Eskimos in the Arctic Circle.

Interestingly, television also helped me realize that being Chinese wasn't bad. As a child I loved watching television, especially superhero shows. On Friday nights at seven o'clock, the Green Hornet was a special guest in our home. With a large bowl of potato chips cradled on my lap and a tall glass of pop in my hand, I anxiously waited to see the Hornet defeat another sinister villain. The Green Hornet was a pretty neat superhero, all right. However, the character I liked most was his trusty sidekick, Kato.

Kato was "super nifty"—and he was Chinese. Kato did not say much, but as a karate expert, he spoke volumes with his hands and feet. He could break doors, chop bricks in half, and render bad guys helpless with his bare hands. Kato made it "nifty keen" to be an oriental.

My classmates also liked watching the Green Hornet and Kato in action. Suddenly, lots of guys wanted to be my friend. They also wanted me to teach them karate. Although I didn't know anything about martial arts, I acted as if I did. I would do a few "impressive" swipes and kicks through the air to give onlookers the idea that I knew what I was doing. The girls in my class would "ooh" and "ah," smiling warmly when I passed them in the hallway. The boys showed me greater respect than before. I'm sure it helped my cause when I told them that Kato (played by Bruce Lee) was a personal friend of mine and that he would beat up anyone who did not treat me right. (You must remember, I wasn't a Christian yet!) Television is indeed a powerful cultural communicator.

International Business

The expansion of the international business community has also helped shrink our world. The United States was once the key player in the world of business, but that is no longer true. Today, there exists what can be termed an international business interdependence. World trade, inflation and deflation, monetary stability and instability, and worldwide economic development are now influenced by and interrelated with the economies of many other countries.

I have had the privilege of visiting and ministering in many countries in Africa and Asia. Fifteen years ago, a McDonald's or KFC restaurant would have been unheard of in many foreign countries. I remember dreaming about eating an order of McDonald's french fries when I first arrived in Zimbabwe, Africa, nineteen years ago. I felt as though I were having withdrawal symptoms because I missed them so much! But you will find many "American" restaurants scattered throughout Africa today. I can now eat McDonald's french fries and Big Macs in Canada, South Africa, Singapore, the Philippines, the Netherlands and many other countries of the world.

We are seeing the globalization of many businesses that were once found only in the United States. The converse is also true. Individuals from all over the world come to America to do business, buying American businesses and investing in American stocks. The auto industry is globalized also. Alongside the Fords and Chevrolets, Buicks and Chryslers on the highways you drive every day, you'll find Toyotas and Mitsubishis, Hondas and BMWs.

My son Matthew and his fiancée Wendy bought a stuffed toy for me as a Christmas present. Eeyore, the sad, droopy-eyed donkey from the Winnie the Pooh stories, is very cuddly. As I was removing tags from one of his ears, I noticed that one tag stated he was made in China. Equally interesting were the tags attached to Eeyore's backside—explaining various things about him in three languages: English, Spanish, and French.

Presently I live in Indiana, where I have visited stores owned and operated by Africans, Koreans, Russians, Chinese, and Spaniards. I enjoy being able to browse in stores that feature African clothing and furniture, Spanish jewelry, Jewish woodcarvings, or Indian silver and brass ornaments.

In recent years, ethnic restaurants also have been on the rise in my area. The other day I counted seven Chinese restaurants in the town where I live. I also counted five Mexican restaurants and nine Italian restaurants.

Politics

While watching the news on television or reading newspapers, one cannot escape the reality that many people live in great poverty. To escape poverty is one reason immigrants stream into more prosperous countries. They believe they will find employment in the new land.

While I was ministering in South Africa during the early 1990s, many people from Hong Kong arrived. They were willing to do any kind of work they could find. Some sold watches on street corners. Others worked as janitors or waiters. Many did manual labor, such as digging trenches for pipe and electrical lines. One immigrant confided to me, "It is better for us to be doing work that may seem menial and unimportant than for us not to be working at all. We are just glad to be in a country where there are jobs for us."

Political persecution has also brought us into contact with individuals from other countries. A short time after World War II, political leaders in the United States began to permit war refugees to enter the country. Later, those who were victims of the Korean conflict and the Hungarian revolt were also permitted into the country. In 1985, *Time* magazine reported that from 1961 to 1984 over a million refugees and immigrants came to the United States from Cuba, Laos, Vietnam, Russia, Cambodia, China, Taiwan, Romania, Poland, Czechoslovakia, and Spain.[2]

Because I have ministered in Cambodia, my ears and eyes are always on the alert for Cambodians now living in the United States. The majority of those I have met say they came here to escape Pol Pot and the Khmer Rouge. Some Chinese who are now living in North Carolina came here to get away from the tyrannical regime of the Communists.

THE IMPLICATION OF CROSS-CULTURAL CONTACT

Increased mobility, advances in technology, the growth of international business, and changing politics have resulted in the expansion of cross-cultural contact. The idea of a shrinking world is not something that should arouse fear. Instead, it should be seen as an opportunity for growth and evangelism.

The Church cannot ignore the reality of globalization. Technology and mobility have facilitated cross-cultural contact, and the Church also must make wise use of these resources. To be faithful to the Great Commission, we must realize that we are called to reach out to persons from other cultures so that *every tribe and nation* might know the love of Jesus Christ.

CASE STUDY: EYE CONTACT

During the Sunday school hour at a church I visited, the class discussion turned to the subject of nonverbal communication. One person raised her hand and bluntly stated, "People should look you straight in the eye when they speak to you. If they do not, it means that they are sneaky and have something to hide. I don't trust people who do not have the courage to look at me when we are talking."

I raised my hand to comment. "In many cultures of the world, looking someone straight in the eye is a sign of rudeness," I said. "The way to show respect is to lower one's eyes when speaking to another. As an Oriental, this is what I was taught. It is not necessarily a sign of deceit. Instead, it can be a sign of respect."

The person who had made the comment muttered, "Well, this is America. If foreigners want to live here, they need to learn how to do things the *right* way!" How would you have reacted to the statement that people are sneaky if they don't look you in the eye?

To Think About . . .

1. Should people who live in the United States or Canada try to "act American" or "act Canadian"? Why or why not?
2. How do you feel when you have contact with people of other cultures? Interested? Nervous? Fearful? Why do you think you feel as you do? Why do you think some people are afraid of cross-cultural contact?

3. Describe the ways that technology and the global economy have affected your life.
4. Describe your most recent contact with someone from another culture?
5. Since it seems inevitable that we (the people of North America) will have increased contact with people from other countries, how should we react to them?

Chapter Two

Understanding Culture

Anthropologists and social scientists once predicted that people of all races would become assimilated and acculturated to such an extent that people would symbolize a melting pot. . . . The melting pot theory is losing ground. The new terminology refers to the mix of people in the workplace as a salad bowl. Emphasis for now and in the future is being placed on valuing the distinctive differences of people.

—Annette DeLavallade, *Melting Pot to Salad Bowl*

As the world shrinks, increasing our opportunities for cross-cultural experience, we must understand the common denominators of culture. What exactly is culture? Let me offer a working definition: Culture is a socially learned system of knowledge and behavioral patterns shared by a certain group of people. In other words, it is a way of life to which a particular society adheres. Six basic concepts are important for understanding culture.

CONCEPT ONE: CULTURE IS SHARED

Culture is a shared set of ideals, values, and standards of behavior that a group claims as its own. Food is a cultural common denominator, so let's pose this question: What do you like to eat?

Perhaps you answered by saying "pizza" or "steak and potatoes." These are the typical answers I receive from American students in my cultural anthropology classes. Their answers demonstrate that they have shared tastes. However, if I were to ask students from another culture what they like to eat, they would almost certainly offer different answers. In my travels around the world, I have learned a lot about dietary preferences. For example:

Eskimos like to eat whale meat.

Japanese like to eat raw fish.

Some in France like to eat frog legs and preserved bumblebees.

African Bushmen like ants, lizards, and ostriches.

The Semang of Malaysia like bamboo rats and monkeys.

The Sotho tribe of South Africa used to eat cats.

Some Asians eat dogs.

The Xhosa tribe of Africa used to eat horsemeat.

The Khmer eat an insect that is a part of the cockroach family, as well as roasted snakes and fried spiders.

The Shona of Zimbabwe eat caterpillars.

Many tribes in Africa like to eat field mice, sugar cane rats, and the intestines of certain animals.

Some Chinese like to eat fish so fresh it is still moving when served.

Whenever I share this with fellow Americans, I usually hear "Yuck!" or "Gross!" in response. I have taught my students that it is inappropriate to use those kinds of responses. Instead, they should learn to say something like "Interesting!"

Some Africans also like to eat flying ants. During the rainy season, the rains come hard and heavy. The run-off then fills the holes in the ground where a certain type of ant makes its home. In order to save themselves from drowning, the ants crawl to the surface, spread their wings, and begin to fly. At times there are so many of them that it actually looks like a blizzard. (The only difference is that when they hit the windscreen of a car, they leave a greasy mess.)

Flying ants are attracted to light. Because of this, they will congregate around municipal lights at night. This is a wonderful time for Africans, because Africans think flying ants are delicious. They are also a great source of protein. The Africans grab large plastic bags, go to the lamp poles, and collect ants. When children have an urge for a snack, they take some of the ants, pull their wings off, and pop them into their mouths.

You are probably wondering, "Jim, have you ever tried eating them?" I have, but not in the raw form (call me "chicken" if you want). My boys and I placed the ants in a bowl of water to remove their wings quickly. Then we fried them until they were crispy and light brown in color. We sprinkled salt over them, and *then* we ate them. They were surprisingly good! What do they taste like, you ask? A bit like potato chips, pretzels, and peanuts all mixed together. I will admit that the first time I ate flying ants, I was a little bothered by those beady little eyes staring at me before I popped them into my mouth!

CONCEPT TWO: CULTURE IS MADE UP OF NORMS

These cultural food preferences may make some readers a little queasy. It's important to remember, however, that some of the foods we eat in America may be just as strange to other people. What we like and dislike are often based on what we are used to—things that seem *normal* to us.

Sonny and Annie Makusha had invited my family to their home for meals on numerous occasions. Annie always prepared a variety of African dishes for us to eat. Her sadza was delicious. (Sadza is a thick cornmeal porridge.) She also cooked goat liver wrapped in intestines, and simmered in thick peanut gravy.

Trust me, it is yummy.

To reciprocate their hospitality, Roxy invited them to our house for a traditional American meal. And to our way of thinking, what could be more American than pizza? Roxy can make a mean, thick-crust pizza with all the toppings. Just thinking about it makes my mouth water!

When the Makushas came to our house, we gathered around the table, said a prayer of thanksgiving, and prepared to dig in. "Sonny," I said. "Since you are our guest, we would like you to serve yourself first."

I waited for him to take a slice of pizza. Instead, he just sat there staring at it. My boys and I could not understand his reaction. "Sonny, go ahead. Help yourself to a slice. You'll like it," I promised.

Sonny continued sitting there, looking skeptically at the pizza. I decided I had to do something. "Sonny, let's go to the living room."

Once we were by ourselves I asked, "Sonny, why don't you want to eat the pizza Roxy made?"

Addressing me with a traditional title meaning *teacher* or *pastor* he said, "Umfundisi, look at it!" as if what he saw was obvious to me.

Did I miss something? I went back to the table and took a good look at the pizza. It looked fine to me, so I returned to the living room where Sonny was waiting for me. "Sonny, I don't see anything wrong with it. In fact, it looks and smells wonderful."

"But Umfundisi, take a really good look at it."

To humor him, I again went to look at the pizza. Roxy gave me a questioning look. My boys grinned, which I understood to mean they were hoping Sonny would decide not to eat the pizza, leaving it all for them. (They love pizza. In fact, one year we had pizza for our Christmas meal.) I again looked at the pizza. Like a scientist, I examined it very closely. What did Sonny see that I was not seeing? Was there a bug stuck to the gooey cheese? After a few moments, I decided nothing at all was wrong with it.

Traipsing into the living room for the third time, I told him, "Sonny, I've looked the pizza over, and it looks fine to me. Come on. If we wait much longer, the pizza is going to get cold."

"Umfundisi, I'm not sure I can eat your pizza," Sonny said at last. "It looks as though it has been chewed and spit out again."

I had never quite thought of pizza that way. My family and I enjoy eating pizza because we have grown up eating it. But pizza was something entirely new for Sonny. It hadn't developed into a norm for him—because it wasn't something he was used to.

CONCEPT THREE: CULTURE IS LEARNED

We are not born with an instinctive knowledge of culture. Instead, we learn culture. Passing culture from one generation to the next is called *enculturation*.

We have all been enculturated into a certain culture. For example, sleeping as a way to replenish the physical body is a biological need. However, the way people sleep is culturally learned. In many rural Japanese homes, people sleep on the floor with a small block of wood for a pillow. Many African villagers sleep on straw mats with no pillow at all. Most Americans like to sleep on mattresses with nice fluffy pillows.

My brother-in-law has a water bed. He was convinced I would really enjoy sleeping in this water bed. Since I had heard a lot of good things about water beds, I looked forward to the experience. Was I ever disappointed! As I crawled onto the bed, I immediately felt as if a gigantic monster were slowly swallowing me alive. All night long, I was tossed back and forth and even felt seasick.

From this experience I drew a conclusion: I prefer a hard mattress to sleep on. It feels a lot more secure. Why did I make this conclusion? Because when I was growing up, I remember hearing my parents talk about the importance of sleeping on a firm mattress to prevent back problems.

CONCEPT FOUR: CULTURE IS INTEGRATED

Culture is integrated, meaning that the different aspects of culture function as a blended whole. Let me illustrate with a few hypothetical situations.

Situation A. You enter a crowded room to attend a meeting. Upon entering the room you look for a place to sit, but you notice that all the seats are already taken. Would you sit on the floor? Why or why not?

Situation B. You are at the airport waiting to board a connecting flight. While you are waiting, you hear that all flights have been canceled because of snow. The earliest flight you can catch is scheduled to leave the next morning. Because of the poor weather conditions, you are stuck at the airport. Would you sleep on the floor? Why or why not?

Situation C. You are at the mall with your child. As you walk through the food court, your little one says, "I want a pretzel." Being kindhearted, you buy a thick, hot, salted pretzel to share. You break off a piece and give it to your child. As he reaches out to grab it, it slips out of his fingers and lands on the floor. Would you pick up the pretzel and eat it? Why or why not?

The majority of Americans would not sit on the floor at a meeting, sleep on the floor at the airport, or eat food that has fallen on the floor. That's because many Americans believe that floors are dirty. Their behavior reflects what they believe. They fill their homes with couches, rockers, bar stools, recliners, tables, and beds. The purpose of this furniture is to keep themselves and their possessions off the dirty floor.

Asians, on the other hand, believe that floors are neither clean nor dirty. Therefore, floors may be used for all kinds of things. When I ministered in Cambodia, I was frequently invited to share meals in people's home. It was considered normal to sit on the floor eating from dishes that were also placed on the floor.

Those who attend the Bam Chum Pun Wesleyan Church sit on the floor during worship services. The floor there serves many functions. Children use it as a desktop for coloring pictures and writing notes. Mothers use it as a bed for their sleeping babies. Men use it as a table for their steaming bowls of tea.

Fashion is another cultural factor. I have heard many young men at the university where I teach say, "I want to date a slim girl." The implication is clear! Being thin is a requirement for being beautiful. One woman told me that most people in America consider Barbie to be the ideal; that is, for a woman to be beautiful, she should be shaped like a Barbie doll. As a result, many young girls starve themselves trying to meet this ideal.

However, this same perception of beauty is not held by all cultures of the world. In certain parts of Africa, a married woman is considered beautiful when she is large, or at least pleasantly plump. (I can almost hear some American wives saying, "Honey, let's go to Africa!") Can you guess why? Many Africans believe that a large married woman is evidence that her husband is a good provider. A skinny wife demonstrates that the man is lazy and not properly taking care of his family.

CONCEPT FIVE: CULTURE IS NOT STATIC

Cultures do not remain the same. Over time they do change. Indeed, they are continually evolving. Some of the most obvious changes in our culture have involved clothing.

When I was growing up I wore a bow tie. It was the "in" thing to do. By my teenage years, however, anyone seen wearing a bow tie was considered a bit "dorky." During my college years, being "cool" meant wearing a wide, striped tie. In fact, as I look at some of the ties I wore during my freshman year in college, I think they look like bibs that babies wear to keep food from spoiling their cute baby clothes.

When I became a youth pastor, ties again changed. The fad was to wear very thin, plain-colored ties. In fact, some of my ties were so skinny it almost seemed like I was wearing a shoestring around my neck. When I returned to America after serving overseas for many years, I realized that ties had changed again. They now had a rounded look to them. Instead of being striped, some looked as if they had been splattered with different colors of paint.

Wearing ties with cartoon characters is one way of being "with it" today. In fact, at Christmas my pastor wore a tie with a picture of Santa Claus. Another friend wore a tie that played a Christmas song when you pressed Rudolf the Reindeer's glowing nose. Perhaps this reflects my upbringing, but I would not advise someone headed for a job interview to wear a tie with Bugs Bunny or Daffy Duck on it!

The changing of styles does not occur only with men's ties, of course. The entire range of men's and women's fashions is a major indicator of cultural direction. Consider the length of dresses. They have gone from long, to short, to shorter, to very short, back to long again. We've all heard the advice, "Keep your clothing, even if it seems to be out of style. Give it a few years and it will be back in style again." That's one of the reasons we say that culture is not static.

CONCEPT SIX: IDEAL CULTURE AND REAL CULTURE ARE NOT THE SAME

What we think we see does not always match reality. Traveling through a desert, we may think we see water ahead. What we are really seeing might be a mirage, an optical illusion. The difference between ideal culture and real culture can be much the same. *Ideal culture* is how people of a certain group perceive themselves or how they describe their way of life to others. *Real culture* is how that group actually operates—how it translates its beliefs and feelings into day-to-day living. The problem arises when ideal culture and real culture do not match.

The other day I overheard two individuals talking about the rules of the road. One woman said, "Indiana has excellent drivers. The drivers in Indiana are nothing like the drivers in New York. New York drivers are horrible. They never obey the rules. We Hoosiers always obey the rules."

On my way home half an hour later, I came to a four-way stop. I slowed my car and came to a full stop, noting that another car was approaching the inter-section. Since I was there first, I assumed the other car would stop and wait for me to go first. Instead, the other car sped through the intersection without even slowing down. I was upset. As my adrenaline surged, I honked the car horn. I was quite surprised by the other driver's response. Not only did he stick his tongue out at me, but he also gave me an unfriendly hand signal. As he drove past, I noticed by his license plate that he was an Indiana driver. So much for the idea that all Hoosiers obey the rules of the road!

We see the same phenomenon with posted speed limits. Our ideal cultural perception is that drivers always obey the posted speed limits. The cultural reality, however, does not match the ideal. The other day as I drove on an interstate highway, I noted the posted speed limit of sixty-five miles per hour. According to my speedometer, I was driving at sixty-eight miles per hour, yet cars were impatiently passing me. Some were going at least eighty miles per hour!

Does this inconsistency between real and ideal culture occur in the Church? Yes, it does. Many churches *seem* to be very interested in missions. Often, the people of the church will talk excitedly about their mission fields in Africa, India, Brazil, or Indonesia. Their ideal culture pictures them as involved, caring, and pro-active. However, the real culture of many churches is that most people ignore the mission field right next door to them. The real does not always match the ideal.

CASE STUDY: SHOULD MEN HOLD HANDS?

Not long after I arrived in Africa, I was scheduled to meet Umfundisi Fayndi Nyoni (then district superintendent of The Wesleyan Church in Zimbabwe) on a chilly Saturday morning. We were going to discuss the affairs of the Bulawayo Zone. According to prior arrangements, we were to meet in front of the Matopos Bookstore.

As I approached the store, I could see that Umfundisi Nyoni was waiting for me. We greeted each other, then decided to go to a nearby cafe to talk. As we began walking, he took my hand and held it tight. Hand in hand, we walked along the crowded sidewalk.

On another occasion, I took nine university students to New York City to show them how ministries can operate in an urban setting. We stayed with people of many races and social backgrounds for two weeks, all living in close proximity.

One day we were invited to a birthday party in President Park. Upon arrival, we were met by our hosts. After greeting us, they proceeded to take our hands and walk us to the place where the food was being barbecued. Having been through this before, I was quite amused by my students' reactions.

Thad told me that when one of the men grabbed his hand, he began to sweat. In fact, as he put it, "My hands were dripping wet, I was so nervous."

Kiel shared, "Having another man hold my hand made me feel very self-conscious. Even though he was talking to me, I did not hear a word he was saying. All I could think was, 'What will other people think?'"

When I asked Thad and Kiel why they reacted the way they did, they replied, "Because we have been taught that men do not hold each other's hands." How would you respond if someone of the same sex held your hand? Why do you think men from certain cultures hold hands? Why do Americans consider this odd?

To Think About . . .

1. Have you ever been invited to eat food that was not familiar to you? How did you react? Why do you think you responded in this way?
2. What might clothing styles tell us about the values of a particular culture?
3. If you were living in Africa, where a plump wife indicated a husband's success and a skinny wife indicated his failure, how would you feel? Explain.
4. List some cultural norms that have changed in your lifetime.
5. Give some examples that show the difference between ideal culture and real culture?
6. What could you do to gain more comfort at being exposed to the norms of other cultures?

Chapter Three

Appreciating Diversity

There is intrinsic value in every human person. Unity becomes all the more important and beautiful in light of the wide ranges of difference in personality, culture, race, gender, talents, and perspectives. Loving each other eliminates devaluation and deprivation of life to one another.

—The Wesleyan Church, Core Values

I believe most Christians want to share the message of God's grace, love, and salvation with others. I often hear believers say, "We want to reach people with the good news about Christ." Not only is this commendable, it is our mandate. Many outside the "fold" desperately need to hear the salvation message.

We must acknowledge, however, that many of the unreached in North America are culturally or ethnically different from the white, middle-class folk who populate most churches. If Christians in North America are to reach people of different ethnic backgrounds, it is imperative that we become cross-culturally sensitive.

"Jim, I hear what you are saying," one believer told me, "but I just do not know where to start. What do I say? What do I do? How can I reach people who are so different from me—different in how they think, how they talk, how they live?"

These are good questions. In fact, I've asked them myself. There was a time when I had to overcome my own prejudices in order to appreciate racial and cultural diversity.

OVER COCONUT CREAM PIE

When I entered Knox College as a freshman, I was assigned to live on the same floor with Scott, a Japanese-American student. You may be thinking that this should have posed no problem for me. Aren't the Chinese and the Japanese pretty much the same? They look the same, right? They all have the same small eyes. (At least, that's what I heard all the time growing up.)

But I saw the Japanese as enemies of the Chinese. During World War II, the Japanese reportedly did horrendous things to their Chinese prisoners. My mom remembers Japanese soldiers entering the village where she lived and mistreating people. All through my childhood I was told that the Japanese were rude, cruel, uneducated, and crude. (Interestingly enough, I later learned that Japanese prisoners reported cruel treatment by their Chinese captors.) As you might guess, I did not want to associate with the Japanese. They were my enemies.

When I found out that a Japanese student was going to be one of my suite mates, I quickly went to the student development office to try to change my room assignment. However, the college administrators did not understand my feelings. Their comments downplayed my very real concern. "If any two people should be able to get along with one another," they said, "it should be you two. You both come from the same part of the world, and you both look the same!"

Steaming with anger, I headed back to the dorm. I was stuck.

For weeks I avoided any contact with Scott. When he was sitting in the lounge, I would stay in my room. During those times when I could not avoid him, I grunted a quick "Hi" and went on my way. I perceived Scott as my enemy. Others may have thought we were alike, but he was Japanese and I was Chinese. As far as I was concerned, we were as different as sushi and sweet and sour pork!

During that first year of college, I attended a community church. The pastor often preached that we should love others, even if they were our enemies. One of his statements really caught my attention. He said, "The Christian's only method of destroying his enemies is to love them into being his friends."

At first I rebelled against the idea of loving my enemies—*especially Scott.* I continued to avoid him. But one Friday night he and I were the only ones left in the dorm. Everyone else had either gone out or gone home for the weekend. Scott came to my room and shyly asked, "Do you want to do something together? I'm going to the restaurant up the street to get some coconut cream pie. I'll pay for yours if you want to come."

You must understand that I have a weakness for coconut cream pie! There was no way I was going to turn down Scott's offer. We walked to the restaurant in silence. Once there, Scott gave the waitress our order: "Two big slices of coconut cream pie and two large glasses of milk, please."

As we waited for the waitress to return, we sat in awkward silence. However, once the food was served and we began to eat, something wonderful took place. We began to communicate. At first our conversation focused mainly on the pie.

"Wow! Is this ever good! I could eat a whole pie all by myself."

"I love coconut cream pie, especially when it is covered with thick, rich whipped cream."

But soon our conversation began to go in all different directions.

"What are you majoring in?"

"Who is your favorite teacher?"

"Which teacher bores you the most?"

"Where are you from?"

"Tell me about your family."

"Do you have a girlfriend?"

By the end of the night, I found myself enjoying Scott's company. He was not rude, uneducated, or cruel. He was not my enemy. In fact, Scott and I had quite a few things in common—the most important was that we were both brand-new Christians. In time, our friendship grew until we became the best of friends.

Through that experience I discovered something the Bible has said all along—God made all people and loves them equally, different though they may be. Cultural and racial diversity are not to be feared; they are good things.

DIVERSITY IN THE OLD TESTAMENT

The Bible is the best place to start in learning how to deal with cultural diversity. Its pages are rich with examples of God's love for variety and His reasons for creating it. Cultural diversity and the proper response to it are thematic threads woven all through the Scripture. Let's begin with the Old Testament.

Creative Diversity

The first chapter of Genesis recounts the story of Creation. God created many things, and they varied greatly. Proof of this is all around us.

I was sitting in my office one day when the first snowflakes of the season began to float gently past my window. Like a small child I ran outside because I wanted the first snowflakes to fall on me. As they began to speckle my dark gray winter coat, I admired the intricacy of each snowflake. Closely examining them, I remembered my junior high science teacher saying that no two were exactly the same. He was right—to this day I have not found two identical snowflakes.

Genesis teaches me that diversity is a demonstration of God's creativity. Since God is the author of diversity, it cannot be a bad thing. How do I know this? Look at Genesis 1:31, which says God declared that all He had created was "very good." Duane Elmer writes that the reason it was very good is creative diversity helps us "begin to capture the character, grace, and glory of God."[1] Elmer is right. A creation of sameness cannot fully portray God's glory.

The Stubborn Prophet

W. Ralph Thompson contends that in no other Old Testament book is God's love and concern for all peoples of the world more beautifully revealed than in the book of Jonah.[2] God commanded Jonah to go and preach to the Ninevites. He wanted the people of Nineveh to repent, since His judgment was imminent. But Jonah disobeyed. He became a stubborn prophet who argued with God and even tried to run away from Him. Jonah boarded a ship that was bound for Tarshish, a city far from Nineveh.

You may already know what happened next. Soon after the boat set sail, God sent a fierce storm. Jonah was thrown overboard and was swallowed by a great fish. As Jonah lay in the belly of the fish in complete darkness, he learned an important lesson—one cannot hide from God or run away from Him. After three days the fish vomited Jonah onto dry land. A battered but wiser Jonah at last headed for Nineveh.

Yet Jonah went reluctantly and with a bad attitude. Nineveh was not only the capital of the Assyrian Empire, but its formidable army had conquered much of the then-known world. This same army was moving closer and closer to the border of Israel, threatening Israel's comfort and peace. An ardent patriot, Jonah hated Ninevites. They were different from the Israelites; they spoke differently, thought differently, lived differently, and worshiped a different God. So instead of preaching to the Ninevites with compassion, Jonah preached with anger.

He went through the right motions, of course. He urged the people of Nineveh to repent. But in his heart, he hoped they would not. He wanted them to feel the full wrath of God's punishment and he wanted to see them destroyed.

But the Ninevites did repent, and God, in His loving mercy, spared them from judgment.

Still hoping that God would destroy the city, Jonah went up on a hill, sat down, watched, and waited. As he watched the city, the sun rose and beat down on him. He became uncomfortable. Sweat rolled down his forehead and into his eyes. His outer garment became soaked.

Then God caused a vine to grow, shading Jonah from the sun. But just as a very glad Jonah was beginning to feel comfortable, God sent a worm to destroy the vine. Jonah's happiness quickly turned to anger, which God soundly reprimanded.

When I first read this account, I did not understand why God would destroy the plant. Then I realized that God did this to teach Jonah a valuable lesson. You see, if Jonah could become angry over the destruction of an insignificant vine, why shouldn't God be passionately concerned about the welfare of the Ninevites? He told Jonah, "You have been concerned about this vine, though you did not tend it or make it grow. . . . Should I not be concerned about that great city?" (Jon. 4:10–11).

The Ninevites may have been ethnically and culturally different from the Israelites, but they were still precious to God. The story of Jonah teaches us that God cares about all people—no matter how different they are from one another.

Israel—A Blessing to All Nations

From the beginning it has been God's intention to bring salvation to all people. God chose to do this through the nation of Israel. According to Genesis 12:3, all nations are to be blessed through Israel. The Israelites were to be priests to all nations. Exodus 19:5–6 states: "If you obey me fully . . . you will be for me a kingdom of priests." What a wonderful thought!

The word *priest* in Latin means bridge builder. Priests are bridge builders in that they connect people to God. They represent God to people and people to God. In the Old Testament we see that God called the entire Israelite nation to be priests—to serve the people of other countries. Through them all men and women of the earth would come to know the true God of the universe.

God called one people to Himself—Israel. But through that people He intended to bless every nation of the earth. All peoples are included in God's plan of salvation.

DIVERSITY IN THE NEW TESTAMENT

The New Testament also contains many passages that deal with cross-cultural issues. John Oxenham sums them up in his well-known hymn, *In Christ There Is No East or West*.

> In Christ there is no East or West,
> In Him no South or North;
> But one great fellowship of love
> Thro'out the whole wide earth.

Jesus' Family Tree

Matthew, a first-century Jew, begins his Gospel in a way that may seem odd to Westerners. Before launching into Christ's story, he presents a lengthy genealogy. For a long time I viewed this genealogy simply as a long, boring list to be endured. For Matthew's Jewish readers, however, identifying Christ's heritage at the outset was the natural thing to do. The Jews found the record of names interesting because, to them, understanding a person's ancestry was essential to understanding that person's life.

As I researched Christ's genealogy, I was intrigued by the comments of William Barclay. He wrote:

> The barrier between Jew and Gentile is down. Rahab, the woman of Jericho, and Ruth, the woman of Moab, find their place within the pedigree of Jesus Christ. Already the great truth is there that in Christ there is neither Jew nor Greek. Here, at the very beginning, there is universalism of the gospel and of the love of God.[3]

The word *universalism* may confuse some people. It might cause them to wonder, "Is Barclay saying that everyone will be saved because of God's love?" That is not what the writer is saying at all. To Barclay, *universalism* means that God's gift of salvation is offered to everyone on this earth, but people must still make the decision to accept the offer.

The genealogy of Christ shows that God wants to include all types of people in His family.

Universal Love

When I was eighteen years old, my high school friend Andy opened his Bible and asked me to read John 3:16. I carefully and slowly pronounced the words that had been placed before me: "For God so loved the world that he gave his one and only Son, that whoever believes in him shall not perish but have eternal life." As I read, I thought, "Wow! How beautiful!"

It was wonderful to realize that God does not love only certain people, but all the people of the world. His love is so great that He sent His Son, Jesus, to die a cruel death on a rugged cross so that people from "every tribe and language and people and nation" could be included in His plan of salvation (Rev. 5:9).

Part of His Team. When I was a boy, I used to *try* to play basketball. When there were enough boys around to form teams, two of them would be elected captains. The captains then selected those they wanted to play on their teams. One by one they called out names: "I want Eddie" or "I want Sam." They would continue to call out names until everyone had been assigned to one of the teams.

Because word had gotten out that I was a lousy player, I was usually not chosen to play at all. However, they were kind enough to soften the blow. "Jim, we have enough for two teams already. Why don't you be our ball retriever? That is a very important job. When there are no balls to retrieve, you can be our cheerleader." Those guys must have figured there's a sucker in every crowd.

Not being chosen for a team made me feel sad, lonely, and left out. Have you ever felt this way? It is not a pleasant experience. However, while others in this world may make us feel left out, God does not. The Bible tells us that He loves us so much that He wants us to be a part of His team!

Loved by God. The idea that diversity is good was quite a revelation for someone like me, who had always been left out, looked down upon, and made fun of for being different. Growing up in New Jersey, my brothers and I were the only Chinese who attended our grade school. We were the only people of color in a sea of white. Even during the time when Kato, the Green Hornet's sidekick, made it "cool" to be Chinese, I could not avoid the stigma of being different. Some of the students at our school would taunt us by yelling things like:

"Look at the Chinks!"

"Why don't you go back to China where you belong?"

"We don't like slant eyes here!"

I hated their taunting. Though I was not a Christian at the time, I remember whining to the Creator, "God, why didn't you make me white like all the other kids in my school? I hate being different."

For years I tried to hide my oriental features. I stayed out of the sun as much as possible in order to avoid having darker skin. I wore sunglasses to hide my small, almond-shaped eyes. I wore a hood when I walked around town to hide my black hair. If it had been possible, I would have dyed my hair blond, surgically widened and straightened my eyes, and obtained blue contact lenses. I felt embarrassed walking with my mother and two brothers because they were Chinese. I hated being Chinese. It did not seem fair to me that God had made me different!

Hearing about God's love changed that.

Whereas the Old Testament creation story helped me realize that it is all right to be different, John 3:16 helped me realize that I am loved! A popular children's song also had a great impact on me, even though I was twenty years old when I first heard it:

> Jesus loves the little children,
> All the children of the world.
> Red and yellow, black and white,
> They are precious in His sight.
> Jesus loves the little children of the world.

Universal Ministry

Peter's experience as detailed in chapter ten of Acts provides another lesson on cultural diversity. Peter had gone to the rooftop of Simon the tanner's home to pray. There he fell into a trance and had a vision that affected the rest of his life. He saw heaven open up and a large sheet with all kinds of animals in it lowered to earth. God commanded Peter, "Get up. Kill and eat" (Acts 10:13).

Incredulous and amazed, Peter cried out, "Surely not, Lord! I have never eaten anything impure or unclean" (Acts 10:14).

For years I thought this passage referred only to food. The Israelites had many rules concerning what they could and could not eat. Some animals were considered clean, while others were considered unclean.

From a medical perspective, I understood why God imposed certain dietary regulations. When I was in the army, I was a preventive medicine instructor at Fort Sam Houston in San Antonio, Texas. I taught recruits the dangers of eating "unclean" food by showing a brief movie about trichinosis. The film clip began by showing a dead pig placed on an operating table. Men dressed in white medical garb then surgically opened its chest cavity. (Although it was incredibly disgusting to watch, the soldiers were so intrigued they couldn't turn away!) As the camera moved in for a close-up, the audience could see hundreds of trichinosis worms trying to crawl their way out of the pig's chest. The recruits quickly and graphically learned the danger of eating improperly cooked pork. The cooking temperature must be high enough to kill the worms. If it isn't, people will ingest them and might become deathly ill.

Peter's strong reaction to God's command to "kill and eat" all kinds of food is understandable because of the culture in which he lived. He was concerned about the cleanliness of what he ate. But there's more to this story. Acts chapter ten is not simply about dietary regulations. Commenting on this passage, Adam Clarke wrote that Peter's revelation was "perhaps intended to be an emblem of the universe, and its various nations, to the four corners of which the gospel was to extend, and to offer its blessings to all the inhabitants, without distinction of nation."[4]

In other words, Peter was being called to minister the gospel to Jews and Gentiles alike. This is made especially clear by the expression, "Do not call anything impure that God has made clean" (Acts 10:15). Jewish prejudice was to be discarded. As Charles Carter wrote, "Prejudice and undue conservatism lock the gates of the Kingdom of God against the world for whose salvation Christ died."[5]

DIVERSE WORSHIP STYLES

Ministering in several different countries has allowed me to participate in worship with various styles. It is very easy to get locked into one worship style. But Revelation 7:9 describes a grand, multicultural, multinational worship service in which people "from every nation, tribe, people and language" will be "standing before the throne and in front of the Lamb." People with diverse backgrounds will be united in worshiping the Heavenly King!

Would I be wrong to speculate that there may still be cultural differences in heaven, or that our heavenly homes may be surrounded by the homes of people from different ethnic backgrounds? It's something to think about.

Labeling Is Not Biblical

Often, we use skin color as a label. We categorize people as white, black, yellow, or red. But the Bible does not use these labels. Instead, it proclaims that God made man in His image (Gen. 1:26–27) and that we are all descendants of the first human couple. All of us are related to each other in the human family. The Bible focuses not on our differences but on our similarities. Because we were all born depraved, we all need redemption and reconciliation. In other words, we are all sinners, and we all require a Savior.

Reuben H. Brooks provides this helpful summary of what the Bible teaches about cultural diversity:[6]

1. The Bible shows no ethnically pure, "correct" culture.
2. We should accept people from every culture and ethnic group as our neighbors and treat them with mutual respect and dignity, as the Bible teaches us to.
3. The Old Testament is replete with examples of a transcultural gospel.
4. The New Testament does not show one culture to be correct and all others to be wrong.

5. To cross into other cultures is the expected norm for God's people, not the exception.

Both the Old and New Testaments demonstrate that God is the author of diversity. He created us with our differences, and loves us all equally. As followers of Christ, then, we must learn to embrace the people of other races and cultures—just as God does.

Conformity Quagmire

Some early missionaries to the Native Americans did not appreciate Native American culture—in fact, they saw it as evil. One Sunday morning when some Native American converts gathered for worship, missionaries told the men, "If you really want to be good Christians, you must cut your hair. Real Christian men have short hair." Some of the Native American converts went to the barber and had their hair cut short.

As the months passed, the missionaries continued to give instructions concerning what it meant to be good Christians. The Native American converts were told, "If you really want to be good Christians, you need to get rid of your robes. You must also get rid of your sandals and wear proper shoes. Good Christians do not show their toes in public."

In order to comply with the new teachings, some of the converts did get rid of their buckskin robes. The men bought "proper" shirts and trousers, and the women bought "decent" dresses. They also got rid of their sandals and bought modest shoes. Those who did not want to follow the teachings simply stopped coming to the Christian meetings.

Eventually, the missionaries told the converts, "If you really want to be good Christians, you need to build a church in which to worship." They reasoned that worshiping God outdoors was disrespectful.

After months of collecting money, gathering materials, and working together on the construction, they completed the church building. With great excitement the believers looked forward to the day when the church would be dedicated. It was going to be a great day, with special singing, a guest speaker, and a feast.

On the day of the dedication, those attending stood outside the church until the ribbon that blocked entry into the sanctuary was cut. As the ribbon floated to the ground, large crowds of Native American believers, dressed in their shirts, jeans, dresses, bonnets, and shoes streamed into the sanctuary and sat down in the pews. As they looked up, they were stunned by a portrait of Christ that had been donated to the new church.

Perhaps you have seen a picture like the one that hung in this church, a picture of Jesus with little children gathered around Him. Although it is a beautiful picture, it really confused the Native American Christians. What they saw seemed to contradict everything they had been taught.

They had been taught that true Christian men had short hair. Yet in the picture, Jesus had long, flowing hair.

They had been told that they should get rid of their buckskin robes and wear "proper" clothes. Yet in the picture, Jesus was wearing a robe.

They had been taught that it was immodest to wear sandals. Yet in the picture, Jesus was wearing sandals in public.

They had been encouraged to build a church, since it was disrespectful to God to meet outdoors. Yet in the picture Jesus, was sitting on a rock—outside—ministering to people.

It is a mistake to believe that everything about a single culture is right or wrong. If we are to reach others with the love of Christ, we must learn to appreciate their diversity and cultural distinctiveness. We must learn to see them as their Creator sees them—through a lens of love.

CASE STUDY: A MATTER OF TRUST

An oriental friend related what happened to him when he accepted a job with a Christian organization. One of his new colleagues took my friend aside and made it clear that he would have to earn the colleague's trust and respect because he had been taught by his father not to trust Japanese people. When my friend dug deeper to discover why his colleague felt this way, he learned that the man's father harbored bitterness because of what the Japanese had done at Pearl Harbor. My friend explained that he was Chinese, not Japanese, that he was not born until many years after World War II, and that he was a loyal American. In fact, he had served in the United States Army! None of that mattered. In the eyes of this associate, my friend was not to be trusted. Have you witnessed instances of prejudice in the workplace? How did you respond?

To think about . . .

1. Why do we often feel threatened by people who are different?
2. Do you think it's true that God intentionally created diversity? Why might He have done that?
3. Are some cultural differences OK while others are not? How can you tell the difference?
4. Why do you think the missionaries in the story wanted the Native Americans to cut their hair and wear European-style clothing?
5. If you had been one of the missionaries, what do you think you would have done? Why?
6. After reading this chapter, are you more or less interested in developing cross-cultural relationships? Why?

Chapter Four

Barriers to Building Cross-Cultural Relationships

The worst danger to real Americanism during the last fifty years has come from foreign ideas and agitators. . . . Certain religious sects that refuse to salute the flag should be forced to conform to such a patriotic action, or else be abolished. . . . Americans may not be perfect, but the American way has brought us about as close as human beings can get to a perfect society. . . . it is only natural and right for each person to think that his family is better than any other. . . . The best guarantee of our national security is for America to have the biggest army and navy in the world and the secret of the atom bomb.

—W.B. Gudykunst and Y.Y. Kim, *Communicating With Strangers*

A barrier is an obstruction. It is something that separates, as a fence separates two houses. It can be a barricade that restricts movement, such as a police roadblock. A barrier implies restriction. This chapter describes the barriers that hinder cross-cultural interaction or predispose people to view those who are different in a negative manner. We will first consider the origins of these barriers, then identify three primary barriers that have hindered many people from having successful cross-cultural interactions.

THE ORIGIN OF BARRIERS

Like culture, barriers are not instinctive. We are not born with them, just as we are not born with specific ideas about culture. Barriers to meaningful relationships with those who look, act, or think differently from us are learned. We learn barriers from three sources.

People

Some barriers are learned from individuals with whom we have frequent contact. Parents, relatives, friends, and school and work colleagues all help to mold how we think and behave.

During my high school years, it was the "in" thing to wear jeans that were stained, faded, and full of holes. Going to school with brand-new jeans was "not cool." Like many of my friends, I did not want to be "uncool." One day my mother bought a new pair of dark blue jeans. "Jim, I noticed that your jeans were in pretty bad shape," she said. "I hope you don't mind, but I threw them away and got you a new pair at Sears."

I groaned inwardly. "Mom, how could you *do* that?" I thought to myself. "I know my old jeans looked bad, but that is how I *wanted* them to look. I can't wear new jeans. If I do, I will never hear the end of it! I will be the laughing-stock of my school!"

Of course, verbalizing my unpleasant and ungrateful thoughts would have gotten me grounded for the rest of my life. So, I smiled politely and said, "Thank you, Mom."

But when she was not looking, I took the new pair of jeans and drenched them with liquid bleach. I then put them on, sneaked outside, and rolled around in a mud hole. The result of mixing bleach and mud into my jeans was wonderful. It made them look old and creatively unique.

Now that I am older and more mature, I can reflect on my actions and chide myself. "Jim, how foolish to have destroyed a pair of new jeans just because you did not want to be ridiculed by your peers." Yet my actions clearly demonstrated my desire to fit into the culture. In order to be perceived as "with it," I allowed others to mold my thinking and actions. The reality is that I am who I am partly because of the input of those who have touched my life. That has some interesting implications, as well. The other day someone said to me, "Jim, I was just talking to your sons. You know, they think so much like you do." Our thoughts and attitudes are shaped by those around us.

Personal Experience

We acquire other barriers from personal experience. One of these barriers is making generalizations about people of a different race or ethnic group.

When I was growing up in East Orange, New Jersey, Puerto Ricans began moving into the neighborhood. I observed that some of the first Puerto Ricans who moved into our apartment building could not speak English very well. Unkindly, I came to the conclusion that all Puerto Ricans were uneducated and poor.

My thinking was that people who could not speak English very well must not be educated. My mother had told me many times that I needed a good education in order to get a good job. If I did not obtain a good job, I would be poor the rest of my life. As you can guess, my generalizations have been proven wrong many times over.

Mass Media

A third way we acquire barriers is through books, newspapers, magazines, movies, television programs, and commercials. These forms of mass media often communicate generalizations about many groups of people.

One movie character I especially hated when I was growing up was Charlie Chan. As far as I was concerned, Charlie Chan was an insult to the Chinese race. Chan epitomized everything that Americans thought to be Chinese. He spoke slowly, using a dumb, falsified Chinese accent, and he wore clothing that no Chinese I knew would ever wear. However, what really angered me was how he addressed his sons. Instead of calling them by name, he would say things like, "Come here, number one son of mine," or, "Go to the police, number two son."

How unrealistic and demeaning! Yet those in my school who were Charlie Chan fans thought that Chan was the "real thing." (To add insult to injury, the actor who played Charlie Chan wasn't even Chinese!) It didn't take long before my fellow students stopped calling me Jim and started referring to me as "Number one China boy." Charlie Chan was no hero of mine. He was an embarrassment!

KEY BARRIERS

Of all the barriers to effective cross-cultural interaction, three are especially destructive. They are ethnocentrism, stereotyping, and prejudice.

Barrier One: Ethnocentrism

In his 1906 book, *Folk-ways*, W. G. Sumner defined ethnocentrism as the view in which one's own culture is at the center and all others are scaled and rated with reference to it.[1] The term comes from two Greek words. *Ethnos* can mean *nation* or *a people*. *Kentro* means *center*. The combination of these two words conveys the picture of individuals who perceive their culture to be the best one and who judge other cultures by the standards of their own culture. Ethnocentrism is the belief that one's own culture is superior to another. It is cultural arrogance. An attitude of arrogance has a way of causing a person to avoid another culture, to withdraw, to make faulty attributions, or to categorize.

Cultural Arrogance. A group of Americans went overseas for some short-term missions work. Before long, they were heard making the following comments to the nationals:

"In America we do things more efficiently than you do here. We arrive at work on time . . . not like you Africans who always arrive late. You need to learn from us."

"We can't eat your food. It may make us sick. Now, if you were visiting us in America, you would not have to worry about getting sick. Our food has been inspected by health inspectors and is therefore very clean."

"We don't buy your clothing because it falls apart too quickly. American clothing is made to last for a long time. It is strong and not weak like your clothing."

"If you really want to get a good education, you should come to America. Our colleges and universities are the best in the world."

Some Positive Aspects. To give the impression that ethnocentrism does not have a positive side would be misleading. A certain amount of ethnocentrism is needed for people to be content with their lives and to ensure that their culture will endure. Positive, mild ethnocentrism results when people hold certain values dear but do not insist that others live by these same standards.

Positive ethnocentrism maintains unity and promotes cohesion among a group of people. In their book *Communicating With Strangers*, W. B. Gudykunst and Y. Y. Kim maintain that ethnocentrism gives groups a greater chance of surviving unwelcome external forces by putting up a united front against those perceived as a threat.[2] The Great Wall of China is a demonstration of this kind of ethnocentrism.

An Equal Opportunity Barrier. Having come in contact with many cultures, I can confidently say that ethnocentrism is found all over the world.

North Americans are ethnocentric. For example, consider the annual event we call the "World Series." During this series, a baseball team from the American League and one from the National League bat it out to see who is the best. The players on the winning side are called "world champs." However, are they really the *world* champions? That is, are they really the best in the world, or are they only the best in North America? If we say that they are the best in the world, then why are teams from countries such as Mexico, Korea, or Japan not invited to participate in the series?

Africans are ethnocentric. The Zulu are considred a major tribe of South Africa. The name *Zulu* comes from a word meaning sky or heaven. The Zulu consider themselves to be the people who come from above. By contrast, the Zulu call another African tribe from Zimbabwe the Shona. The word *shona* means down under, below, or underfoot. The Zulu thus see themselves as being superior (from above) and the Shona as being inferior (underfoot) individuals who are destined to be under the feet of a greater tribe.

Orientals are ethnocentric. While growing up, I was continually told, "Chinese are the best. They are the brightest, the smartest, and the most creative of all the peoples of the world." I was even taught that truly civilized individuals eat with chopsticks, while barbarians eat with their hands or with forks and knives.

Hindus are ethnocentric. Because cows are sacred to Hindus in India, Hindus consider the American practice of eating beef to be both primitive and disgusting. That's not the only thing we do that they think of as disgusting. Read what one ethnocentric Hindu observer of American culture wrote about a certain activity of ours:

> The daily body ritual performed by everyone includes a mouth-rite. Despite the fact that these people are so punctilious about the care of the mouth, this rite involves a practice which strikes the uninitiated stranger as revolting. It is reported to me that the ritual consists of inserting a small bundle of hog hairs into the mouth, along with certain magical powders, and then moving the bundle in a highly formalized series of gestures. In addition to the private mouth-rite, the people seek out a holy-mouth man once or twice a year. These practitioners have an impressive set of paraphernalia, consisting of a variety of augers, awls, probes, and prods. The use of these objects in the exorcism of the evils of the mouth involves almost unbelievable ritual torture to the client. The holy-mouth man opens the client's mouth and, using the above mentioned tools, enlarges any holes which decay may have created in teeth. Magical materials are put into these holes. If there are no naturally occurring holes in the teeth, large sections of one or more teeth are gouged out so that the supernatural substance can be applied. In the client's view, the purpose of these ministrations is to arrest decay and to draw friends. The extremely sacred and traditional character of the rite is evident in the fact that the natives return to the holy-mouth man year after year, despite the fact that their teeth continue to decay.[3]

The Danger of Ethnocentrism. Ethnocentrism becomes objectionable when people believe that their values are the only correct ones and that all people everywhere should be judged by how closely they live up to those values. This breeds intolerant attitudes and behavior. The danger of ethnocentrism is that it may feed its own pride until those who are different are looked down upon with disdain and contempt. One of my
professors at Wheaton College Graduate School once said, "An ethnocentric group responds favorably to itself and unfavorably to others."

Ethnocentrism becomes a barrier to cross-cultural relationships by causing people to become narrow and rigid in the way they think and behave. Carol and Melvin Ember write that ethnocentrism hinders "our understanding of the customs of other people and, at the same time, keeps us from understanding our own customs. If we think that everything we do is best, we are not likely to ask why we do what we do or why 'they' do what 'they' do."[4]

Barrier Two: Stereotyping

The term *stereotype* was coined in 1922 by Walter Lippmann, a public relations expert and writer who was familiar with the printing business. Lippmann knew that in the printing industry a stereotype was a printing plate from which the same image was produced over and over. Today, the term refers to a fixed impression of a certain group of people from which judgements are made by others.

Some common stereotypes—fixed impressions—are revealed by the following statements:

All Orientals are good in math.

All African-American males can jump high and play basketball.

All Americans are rude.

All Jews are tightwads.

All Africans have rhythm and can sing.

All Americans are rich.

All American women are promiscuous.

A Valid Purpose. Richard Brislin contends that stereotypes are necessary to help individuals think and communicate.[5] Every day we are bombarded with millions of isolated pieces of information. In order to make sense out of all this input, we need to categorize the information. That is what we do when we stereotype people. We seek to organize our world. When we refer to policemen, professors, students, or Christians, we are using stereotypical categories to help us evaluate them.

Let us say that you are introduced to a doctor. You do not know anything about him except that he is a doctor. By knowing this little bit of information, you can begin to categorize. You unconsciously assign to him all the characteristics you believe a doctor should possess. Therefore, if you believe doctors should be intelligent, caring, efficient, and rich, you begin to treat him that way.

Negative Consequences. However, I can attest that stereotyping someone in a negative way can have some interesting consequences. While attending my first chapel service after being hired to teach at Indiana Wesleyan University, I found a seat and waited for the service to begin. As I sat there, Jeff sat down next to me and asked, "What country are you from?"

I was a bit surprised by the question. Then it dawned on me that Jeff thought that I was a new foreign student. Because it took me a few moments to figure out how to answer him, Jeff took control of the conversation.

"I guess you did not understand me," he said very deliberately. "I will speak slower. Myy—naame—iis—Jeeff. Whaat—iis—yoouur—naame?"

By now I was dumbfounded, totally shocked at how he was speaking to me. My silence must have spurred him on. This time he spoke even more slowly, upping his volume so that other students were taking notice. I felt insulted at being treated like a child.

What had happened? Jeff's stereotype of Orientals was that they could not understand or speak English. When I was finally able to interrupt him, Jeff was embarrassed and apologetic. With a red face he said, "You can speak!"

He mumbled an explanation: "I have never met an Oriental who could speak good English. I just assumed that you would not be able to understand me."

A Widespread Practice. Virtually all cultures stereotype. Even cultures that appear to be similar are guilty of stereotyping one another. Some Orientals have stereotyped other Orientals. The following quote shows how some Chinese from the People's Republic of China viewed the Japanese:

> A Japanese man is an irrational, brutal, temperamental, and war-loving person, who lives with his hypocritical wife in a miserable small house in a hierarchical, submission-oriented, and feudalistic society, communicating with his fellow men in an inadequate language, while cooperating with the government and big business in the economic, but soon to be military, invasion of other Asian countries, all the while being unconsciously under the influence of the dominantly superior Chinese culture and civilization.[6]

When I taught at a Bible school in Zimbabwe, I gave students this exercise to help them become better acquainted with me. I asked them what they thought about the Chinese. Their answers were very interesting.

"Chinese men grow Fu Manchu mustaches."

"Chinese have cereal bowl haircuts."

"Chinese all have buck teeth."

"Chinese all walk funny."

"Chinese do not show much emotion."

"Chinese are cruel."

Facts About Stereotypes. To have effective cross-cultural interaction, we need to recognize four facts about stereotypes.

(1) Stereotypes can either be positive or negative. For example, some countries stereotype Americans as being friendly, outgoing, hard working, and generous. Some negative stereotypes mark them as boastful, always in a hurry, and wasteful.

(2) Stereotypes vary in intensity. In other words, some people may believe a given stereotype more earnestly than others. Sometimes this intensity is reflected in how individuals articulate what they believe about a certain group. Saying "Blacks are always militant" is a lot stronger than saying "Blacks are militant in certain situations."

(3) Stereotypes vary in accuracy. Statements like "Blacks are untrustworthy," "Native Americas are a bunch of drunks," or "Chinese are sneaks" are oversimplifications and overgeneralizations. The information these stereotypes convey may be accurate in some cases, but certainly not in all cases. Stereotypes may not be entirely wrong. I have met Blacks who have been untrustworthy; I have met Native Americans who did drink too much; and I have met Chinese who were sneaky and dishonest. However, to categorize every individual in a group as being the same is unfair because it is not totally accurate.

(4) Stereotypes may vary in content. All people may not possess the same collection of stereotypes for a given group. Whereas some Americans may criticize Mexicans as lazy, poor, dirty, and unmotivated, other Americans will praise Mexicans for being loyal, cheerful, and passionate. Larry Samovar writes, "Although there are some widely-shared stereotypes, there is considerable variation in the content of stereotypes for various racial, ethnic, and national groups in a large society like America."[7]

The Problem with Stereotyping. Earlier in this chapter, I listed seven commonly heard statements that stereotype people.

Let's take a closer look at the reality behind these statements.

All Orientals are not good in math. I know this because I am an Oriental, and I am horrible in math. I still use my fingers and toes to do a lot of my counting, adding, and subtracting. When I run out of fingers and toes and can't find a calculator, I'm in trouble!

All African-American males cannot jump high and play basketball. Sean, an African American, was a student in one of my classes. On the first day, the students were each asked to share something about themselves. Sean started out by saying, "I am not athletic. I cannot jump high, and I am not a good basketball player. Instead, I like to read, to listen to good music, and to study."

All Americans are not rude. Some can be very rude, but not all. Bonita and Pam work in the religion department office at the university where I teach. They are kind and very caring, and the students love them. Students feel free to approach either Bonita or Pam for counseling or just to share conversation. Pam and Bonita are definitely not rude Americans!

All Jews are not tightwads. To say that money is the only thing Jewish people care about is really offensive, yet I have heard it said many times. In high school, I had a Jewish friend who would have given the shirt off his back to someone in need. In fact, he was probably the most giving person I knew during that period of my life.

All Africans do not have inborn rhythm and the ability to sing. I knew an African pastor who loved to sing. When he got really excited while singing, he would begin to clap. But he definitely was not gifted at either activity. To *love* to sing and to be *able* to sing are two separate things. He was always off-key and could not keep the right rhythm when he clapped. He had a way of messing up a congregational song because he could not clap in unison with the other members of the church. I am certain the Lord appreciated his singing much more than mortal ears did.

All Americans are not rich. Many of the Africans and Asians with whom I've worked believed this stereotype. Because of this, people frequently came to my house asking for money. What was humorous to me was that some of them were actually making more money than I was. However, no matter how hard I tried to explain that I was not rich, they did not believe me. They thought that I was just being stingy and selfish when I did not give them what they wanted.

All American women are not promiscuous. Television, movies, and tabloids have really given the world the wrong image of American women. To say that every American woman is promiscuous would be very far from the truth—no matter what the media portrays.

The problem with stereotypes is that they overgeneralize and oversimplify. This barrier prevents a person from getting better acquainted with individuals from different backgrounds. The glaring and obvious reason that stereotyping is misleading is that the individuals in any group are not identical. It is God's intention that we each be unique.

Barrier Three: Prejudice

In a television interview, Billy Graham was asked what one earthly problem he would most like to change. Without a moment's hesitation, Graham answered that it would be prejudice and racism.

Whereas stereotypes deal with what a person believes, prejudice deals with attitudes and feelings. D.W. Klof defines prejudice as a "negative feeling based upon a faulty and inflexible generalization which may be overt or covert and is directed toward a group of people or toward an individual who is a member of the group."[8] This definition reveals three components of prejudice.

Negative Feelings. Prejudice involves feelings of dislike or hatred towards a group that is perceived to be different. Richard W. Brislin defines prejudice as "a vagrant opinion without visible means of support."[9] European Jews experienced worsening prejudice as the Nazi regime targeted them and deprived them of their rights. Moved from their homes to ghettoes and then to extermination camps, these Jews experienced prejudice of the most cruel and insidious nature. The Star of David they were forced to wear on their clothing, a precious symbol to them, marked them as objects of hatred to others.

Faulty and Inflexible Generalizations. Prejudiced feelings are faulty because they derive from generalizations or prejudgments that are not based on fact. Prejudiced people are inflexible. Even though new information may be presented, the prejudiced person will not change what he or she already thinks and feels. In other words, prejudgments become prejudices when they become irreversible, even in the face of conflicting evidence. In 1792 Mary Wollstonecraft wrote, "Men, in general, seem to employ their reason to justify prejudices . . . rather than to root them out."[10]

Covert and Overt Prejudice. Some people may be prejudiced but are able to hide how they truly feel. They keep their feelings inside by carefully guarding what they say and do. That is *covert* prejudice. For evidence of this, we have only to recall the covert actions of such groups as the Ku Klux Klan in times past. Functioning as upstanding citizens by day, Klansmen performed acts of terror at night, their identities carefully concealed by the sinister robes and hoods they wore.

Others, however, are very open about their feelings. Their prejudice is undisguised and readily observed by others. This is *overt* prejudice. Citing America's constitutional protection of free speech, many hate groups now operate openly. The Internet also has become a breeding ground for such overt cells of prejudice.

Overt acts of prejudice can take five different forms: antilocution, avoidance, discrimination, physical attack, and extermination.

Antilocution is a verbal expression of hate. Individuals who express prejudice in this manner speak negatively about another group to people who are like-minded. This may be done through ethnic jokes, name-calling, or derisive talk. Doing these things feed the prejudicial attitudes of the speakers and hearers.

Avoidance is a bit harsher than antilocution. It occurs when people make a conscious effort to stay away from groups they do not like.

Sam lives in a community that used to be predominantly white. However, in the past few years many Hispanics have moved into his neighborhood. Sam is upset about this. He makes it clear to anyone who will listen how he feels about "them foreigners." For years Sam shopped at the little grocery store near his house. But since more and more Hispanics are buying their food there, Sam has decided to drive to the next town to shop. He states, "I'd rather drive fifteen extra miles than deal with them foreigners."

Discrimination is taking active steps to exclude or deny members of another group entrance to or participation in a given activity. Examples of discrimination are segregation in educational systems, denial of employment, restricted participation in politics, or exclusion from social or recreational activities.

Physical attack, as the name implies, is the physical assault of a member of a group that is seen as different. An example of physical attack is described in this excerpt from a news article:

In December, an Asian-American male was hit with a glass bottle at his business in San Fransico by an inebriated European-American male. The assailant's threats included, "I'm not gonna leave, you . . . gook or Jap or whatever you are. I'm gonna smash your windows and smash you. Go back to wherever you came from."[11]

In his archetypal volume, *The Nature of Prejudice*, Gordon Allport describes the progression towards violence which can occur between different groups:

Members of an "in-group" hold prejudicial attitudes towards the members of another group. The in-group members begin having problems, and they start blaming the out-group. The in-group's attitude towards the outgroup grows negative, expressing itself first as verbal abuse. As tensions continue to mount between the two groups, the out-group is ostracized in some manner, such as being excluded from certain functions in the community. This may then lead to feelings of hatred, which can then lead to acts of violence.[12]

In his book *Intercultural Encounters*, Donald Klopf states that physical attacks tend to occur in places where groups that have negative attitudes towards each other are thrown into close contact with one other. Also, hot weather contributes to the rise of violence.[13]

Extermination is the final way in which people may express prejudice. It is the organized and premeditated destruction of a group of people.

A MATTER OF LEARNING

Recognizing barriers is the first step in eliminating them. The barriers of ethnocentrism, stereotyping, and prejudice are learned behaviors. We are not born with these tendencies. They "rub off" on us through contact with our family, friends, and the mass media.

Ethnocentrism interferes with cross-cultural relationships by ranking people according to their worth. Stereotyping interferes by misleading people into thinking that all people of a certain group are the same. Prejudice, whether overt or covert, undermines cross-cultural relationships by making negative generalizations that are not based on fact.

Because barriers are learned, they can be unlearned, leading to positive interactions with all of God's people.

CASE STUDY: A TASTE FOR CHILDREN

While speaking at a series of revival meetings in Swaziland, I gave an invitation at the end of each service. Many children were there with their parents, and I sincerely urged them to make a decision for Christ by coming to the altar to pray. I told them, "If you come forward, I will pray with you."

Not one person came forward. I felt like a failure. A few days later I shared my feelings with one of the teachers at the Bible college. She began to laugh.

"What are you laughing about?" I exclaimed. "This is no laughing matter!"

She then explained to me that African parents sometimes keep their children under control by threatening them. One way they threaten them is to tell them that if they are naughty, the "Chinese devil" will come and eat them. I didn't realize it then, but one of the stereotypes the Africans in that area had about Chinese was that we liked to eat African children. The reason people did not come to the altar was that they feared that I would grab them and gobble them up! List some stereotypes you have had about other ethnic groups.

To think about . . .

1. What is the difference between ethnocentrism stereotyping, and prejudice? Which do you see as most harmful? Why?
2. What other barriers (not related to race or ethnicity) have you noticed in the workplace, on campus, or in the business world?
3. Describe some examples of stereotyping that are evident on television or in films.
4. Is America enthnocentric? Give your reasons to support your answer.
5. How do you respond when you hear a racial slur or other ethnically insensitive comment?
6. What progress has your social group made in breaking down barriers? In what areas do you see a need for further improvement?

Chapter Five

What Appreciating Cultural Diversity Is Not

Great achievements are not born from a single vision, but from the combination of many distinctive viewpoints. Diversity challenges assumptions, opens minds and unlocks our potential to solve any problem we may face.

—Poster seen in a shopping mall

The Sunday school class I was visiting was supposed to be discussing the topic of salvation. Instead, one middle-aged man was dominating the class with his opinions. His comments went something like this:

I believe that we Christians have too narrow a view about salvation. We say that Jesus Christ is the only way. What gives us the right to push that belief onto other people? I believe that there are many ways to obtain eternal life. What we should be teaching is this: Jesus Christ is one way; Buddha is one way; Allah is one way; and the thousands of Hindu gods are another way. To teach that Jesus is the only way is wrong and too conservative. If we expect to draw people from different ethnic backgrounds into the Church, we need to become more open-minded in our way of thinking.

Since I was only visiting the class, I decided to wait and see what the other class members would say. Surprisingly, no one spoke up. I was amazed and somewhat irritated by this total lack of response.

The outspoken class member, assuming that the silence granted him the right to continue, pointed at me and said, "Ask him. I am sure that he will agree with me."

He directed his next remarks to me. "Don't you agree that if we want to draw Orientals into Christian churches, we need to become more flexible in what we teach?" he asked. "Don't you think it would help if we would preach that Buddha can also get us into Heaven?"

As he spoke, I felt the blood rushing to my head. I am sure I was turning very red (is that where the term Red Chinese came from?). Slowly, deliberately, I quoted John 14:6, a Scripture I had learned years earlier as a new believer: "Jesus answered, 'I am the way and the truth and the life. No one comes to the Father except through me.'"

After the class ended, the teacher made a point of talking to me. "I hope you don't think we all agree with what that man was saying. We have tried to tell him what the Bible says, but he just will not listen. In fact, he tells us to our faces that we are narrow-minded. We feel uncomfortable having him in class, but none of us want to ask him to leave. Maybe someday he will hear something that will change his way of thinking."

I sympathized with the teacher.

This incident reaffirmed my own opinion that there are people who are confused about what it means to appreciate diversity. To remove some of the fog, let's identify four things that appreciating cultural diversity does not imply.

ONE: ACCEPTING ALL THEOLOGIES

We live in an age of theological relativism. In November 1996, Dr. James Dobson reported that about three-quarters of all adults in America reject the notion that there are absolute moral truths.[1] I contend that the belief that the Bible is not absolutely true will result in the belief that Jesus Christ is not absolutely God.

I was visiting homes with an African pastor in a township near Johannesburg, South Africa. We were distributing tracts and getting acquainted with those who lived near the church. At one house the owner said, "I am a Muslim. I believe in Allah. Allah promises to bless me with the gift of eternity."

The African pastor then responded, "That is fine. We are not here to change your religion. However, we would like to invite you to come to our church since we are both really serving the same God. Jesus and Allah are basically the same."

I was stunned. Allah and Jesus Christ are *not* the same! As a Christian I cannot and will not accept the teaching that all gods can lead us to heaven. By faith I accept the biblical truth that Jesus Christ alone can save me—Allah cannot.

Appreciating cultural diversity does not require acceptance of the tenets of the other world religions. While it may be necessary for Christians to understand what other religions teach and preach, we should never see these as alternatives to the fundamental message of the gospel. The Bible presents one way of salvation. Academic missiologist Paul Hiebert contends that Christians, while needing to be culturally sensitive, must avoid the danger of "reducing the Christian faith to subjective human agreements, opening the door for a theological relativism that destroys the meaning of the truth."[2]

TWO: BLIND ACCEPTANCE

An interesting phenomenon sometimes occurs with individuals enter or interact with a new culture—they blindly accept everything about it. Those in missions circles sometimes refer to this as *going native*.

As much as possible, Christians should try to understand, empathize, and identify with new cultures. Jesus Christ set a wonderful example for us in this regard. The Bible states that He emptied Himself. The Son of God became the Son of Man. By sacrificially surrendering Himself, He willingly gave up what He had in order to minister to us. However, even Christ had limits as to how far He would go to identify with the culture of the world. Louis Luzbetak contends that faith sets boundaries for the Christian who is desirous of ministering to those of other cultures, boundaries that include "prudence, reason, and the goals of the apostolate."[3]

Limits are necessary because all cultures have elements that have been tainted by the Fall. All cultures have elements that are evil or have evil associations. These elements cannot and should not be assimilated into Christianity. To do so would lead to syncretism—the fusion of different forms of belief or practice. "The Willowbank Report" (1978) correctly asserts that believers in Christ must learn to "scrutinize all culture, both foreign and local, in light of [Christ's] lordship and God's revelation."[4]

Before Christianity was introduced to Africans, the witchdoctor was regarded as the spiritual leader of the tribe. When people had problems—whether physical, emotional, or spiritual—they visited the witchdoctor for his counsel and magic. This practice has continued into present-day African life. When a baby is born, for example, many African parents still go to the witchdoctor to buy medicine to protect the infant from evil spirits. The medicine is placed in a small pouch and tied around the child's waist. This *muti* pouch might remain tied on the child for up to four years.

I was astonished when one African couple, who professed to be Christians, went to the witchdoctor to buy muti for their child. When I raised questions, I was told, "There is nothing wrong with what we are doing. We are just following African customs." Yes, there *was* a problem, I told them. What they were doing was contrary to the Bible.

Whereas conversion should not de-culturize a person, every Christian must allow his or her culture to come under the scrutiny of the Lord. Those elements of culture that collide with what Scripture teaches must be rejected. In other words, while certain things in any given culture are neither right nor wrong biblically, others clearly contradict what the Bible says. Those who profess to be Christians must spurn these contradictory elements.

THREE: SURRENDERING CORE VALUES

While the Bible reflects cultural flexibility, it also establishes core values that should be nonnegotiable for Christians. These core values, though they may be stated or emphasized differently from denomination to denomination, represent those things on which Christians should never compromise, regardless of the culture they may encounter. The denomination of which I am a part, The Wesleyan Church, has articulated seven such biblically-based core value statements.[5]

Biblical Authority

The Bible is the highest source of written authority for God's plan for His people. It reveals how to live out that plan individually and corporately. Beliefs, practices, and priorities are to be anchored in clear biblical teachings.

Christlikeness

Jesus Christ is the defining feature of God's will for all humankind. In Christ is found the highest and most practical meaning and the clearest example for holy living or godliness. Christ is both example and strength as [we] pursue integrity, excellence, faith, hope, and love.

Disciple-Making

Making disciples is a clear mandate from Christ. This requires a strong focus on evangelism and training in spiritual growth and holy living. Done effectively, this will produce and promote growth and health in and among the churches.

Local Church Centered

The denomination exists in local churches joined together by common beliefs, values, and practices and committed to common mission. Local churches are the most fundamental and strategic points of evangelism and discipleship. The challenge for denominational servant-leaders is to keep finding the best ways to serve and strengthen congregations.

Servant Leadership

Wesleyans respect leadership that is placed over them, while realizing that the authority and effectiveness of spiritual leadership is not primarily bestowed, but earned and manifested by a loving and willing heart of obedience that serves God and mankind gladly. Wesleyans desire to be leaders in serving.

Unity in Variety

There is intrinsic value in every human person. Unity becomes all the more important and beautiful in light of the wide range of differences in personality, culture, race, gender, talents, and perspectives. Loving each other eliminates devaluation and deprivation of life to one another.

Cultural Relevance

Wesleyans are called to serve the present age. The Church respects and builds on its past, without becoming its slave. Wesleyans are "culture informed" for the sake of reaching people for Christ, but not "culture captives" in the sense of surrendering core values, beliefs, and behaviors.

Understanding one's own biblical core values is essential when trying to determine how to interact with others. Appreciating cultural diversity does not mean surrendering one's core values.

FOUR: AN EITHER/OR PROPOSITION

Developing cultural sensitivity is not an either/or proposition. It does not mean accepting one group and rejecting the other. Instead, it is means developing an appreciation for the uniqueness of different groups and accepting each of them in Christian love.

Responding in Fear

Jason liked to run. Sometimes he varied his route as a way of challenging himself, but he didn't count on getting lost one day. Before long he found himself in an African-American neighborhood that was quite different from his suburban neighborhood. He was tired and totally disorientated. Here's how he later described the incident.

I knew that I should ask someone for help, but I was too scared. I had heard stories from others that Whites were not treated well by Blacks who entered their neighborhoods. I thought that if I kept running I would eventually find some landmark that would help me get my bearings back. However, I found nothing. I was exhausted, and I looked a mess. The sun was beginning to set, and I was getting more and more fearful.

By this time I was forced to walk. The bounce in my legs was gone. Behind me I heard a car approach and slow down. The car window began to roll down, and the face of an African American appeared. He was big. I could see that he was wearing a thick, gold necklace, and he had large rings on his fingers.

The sight of this big black man really scared me. Visions of him beating me up flashed through my mind. He began calling out to me. I did not hear what he was saying because my only concern was to get my legs moving so I could get away from him. However, my tired, wobbly legs were not able to outrun his car. Again I could hear his booming voice, "Hey, man! Don't run! It looks to me as if you need help! I want to help you!"

I knew that there was no escape. My legs just were not willing to move into high gear. Slowly I approached the car. "Hey, man," he said kindly. "You're a long way from your neighborhood, aren't you? You really shouldn't be out here. You don't have to be scared of me. I'm the pastor of a nearby church, and I see that you are totally beat. If you want, I can drive you back to your house."

What Jason learned from this experience changed his "either/or" understanding of cultural diversity. He assumed he was in danger of being beaten up. Instead he found Christ ministering to him through someone who did not meet his expectation of what a pastor should look like.

It's Them or Us

A pastor friend of mine stood at the door of my office recently and shared how things in his church were going. At one time more than eighty-five people faithfully attended the Sunday morning worship services. Today, the church averages around twenty. When I asked him why there was such a decline he said:

I will answer by telling you what happened this past Sunday. The church is located in a community that is 21 percent black. Last Sunday, a biracial couple attended our church. He was African American and she was Caucasian. As people exited the sanctuary at the end of the service, I heard one lady telling another how unhappy she was that a black man had come to her church. Her voice was loud enough for many others to hear her comments. I approached her and expressed my disappointment. Without remorse she said, "So, you would rather have them than us!"

MAKING CHRIST RELATIVE

Surrendering to Christ does not mean surrendering all of the things that distinguish us culturally. As we reach out in Christ's name for positive cross-cultural interaction, we must learn to maintain cultural diversity without sacrificing Christian theology.

Christians do not blindly accept everything another culture offers, especially if it contradicts biblical truth. The Apostle Paul became "all things to all men" in order to "save some" (1 Cor. 9:22), but he never compromised the gospel of Jesus Christ.

Core values are an important anchor in the Christian life, holding believers f irmly to essential absolutes in a relativistic world. Developing cultural sensitivity means remaining true to these core values while remaining open to opportunities for spiritual growth that are made available by the rich diversity of the human race.

CASE STUDY: PLAYING IT SAFE

Trying to drum up support for the upcoming elections, an African government leader was making a speech. Perhaps in an attempt to reach as many people as possible, he told the gathered crowd that he was a Christian—and a Muslim, a Buddhist, a Hindu, and an African who believed in ancestral spirits. This man was not willing to take any chances! If the god of one religion could not get him to heaven (or get him reelected), he reasoned that another would. He was simply trying to play it safe.

How have you seen the "play it safe" mentality portrayed in popular culture such as television and movies?

To think about . . .

1. Have you observed some Christians "going too far" in promoting cultural diversity? Explain.
2. Name some ways a church with a predominantly white congregation can develop more cultural diversity?
3. When people who are ethnically or racially different come to a church, how can the church members make them feel welcome?
4. Make a list of your core values, things about which you will not compromise.
5. Can you remember a situation in which you misjudged someone by appearance?

Chapter Six

How to Become Cross-Culturally Sensitive

Successful communication with self and others implies correction by others as well as self-correction.

—Jurgen Ruesch

Contemporary American society is more hospitable to minorities and is more racially egalitarian than it has ever been before. Companies and businesses are making an effort to promote harmony in diversity. An acquaintance of mine told me about a conference she attended for her company. The focus of the week was how to live and work in a world of diversity. She reported, "I was made to think about things that I had never thought about before. It was uncomfortable to examine attitudes I have towards people of different backgrounds. But I am glad I went to the conference. The best part of the week was when they gave us ideas about how we could move towards harmony in the midst of diversity."

In a 1996, Ellis Cose asked the following: "Do we have the vaguest idea how to create a society that is truly race neutral?" In response to his own question, he wrote, "The short answer, I suspect, is no. Otherwise we would be much further along the way than we are."[1]

The Church in America must move beyond platitudes like "as Christians, we love everyone." Someone offered the insight that using platitudes may be just an effort to make ourselves feel good in spite of the fact that we are no closer to solving the problem. The Church must move beyond words to action. Here are ten things you can do to become more cross-culturally sensitive.

ONE: UNDERSTAND YOURSELF

The ways in which we conduct ourselves play an integral role in determining how we perceive others, the way they think, and the way they do things. Our behavior thus determines the success of our interactions with people of different ethnic backgrounds. Our predispositions inform us what is good or bad, right or wrong. They more or less control our conduct as we interact with others.

These predispositions are picked up within the framework of a particular culture. In other words, pre-dispositions are culturally prescribed and, therefore, will vary from one culture to another.

We must understand that people living in countries like the United States or Canada are not monocultured. All of us belong to, or can identify with, a variety of different groups or subgroups. The groups to which we belong change over our lifetime.

Hanging Out

When Tom was in high school, he associated mainly with two different groups. Sometimes he hung around long distance runners, since he was an all-state track and field star. At other times he hung around singers, since he was also a tenor in the all-state choir. Now that Tom is forty-five years old, he no longer hangs around runners or singers. Although he still enjoys running and singing, his time is mostly taken up by work. Now, he associates primarily with people who work in his office or live in his apartment complex.

Finding Your Roots

Ellen Summerfield contends that before being able to relate effectively to people who are ethnically different, one must understand one's own roots.[2] Failure to do so creates severe limitations. Edward Stewart agrees: "From the American's point of view, his own values and assumptions prevent him from objectively perceiving and understanding the underpinnings of the behavior of his counterpart. His performance would be enhanced if he understood both his own culture and that of his counterpart."[3] In other words, understanding our cultural characteristics can help us be more perceptive of our differences from other people. Summerfield explains:

> If you are white, don't make the mistake of thinking that this is "all" you are and that you "have no culture." Because yours is the predominant culture, it may just seem as if you have nothing to distinguish yourself from others. Learn more about your particular brand of "whiteness" as well as about your other cultural identities growing out of your religion, profession, geographical location, and so on. The more you understand about these multiple identities, the more you will realize how cultural stereotypes distort by oversimplifying.[4]

The Benefit of Having Roots

Understanding our own culture benefits us in at least four ways.
(1) It prepares us for the challenges of cross-cultural contact.
  Understanding ourselves makes us more likely to compare and contrast our ways of thinking and doing things with others.
(2) It promotes objectivity in appraising ourselves and others.

(3) It shows us how little we actually understand about other cultures.

(4) It motivates us to learn more about other people and their cultures.

TWO: EMPATHIZE WITH OTHERS

When dealing with people, whether they are ethnically different or not, it is important to empathize with them. Empathy is feeling what another person feels. It is perceiving something as another perceives it. In other words, empathy means looking at situations not just from our viewpoint but from the viewpoint of the other person as well. According to the old adage, it is putting one's self in another's shoes.

One of the greatest barriers to empathy is self-focus. If one is consumed with thoughts of self, it will be almost impossible to focus on others. Someone commented, "If the main focus of our attention is directed towards wondering how much the other person likes our shoes, hairstyle, clothes, or looks, we unquestionably are not in a position to employ much energy in the direction of developing empathy."

It is impossible to see and understand everything from another person's point of view. Yet those who wish to build relationships with people from other backgrounds must try. We do this by developing skills in listening and observing—making a sincere effort to understand the other person's ways of thinking and doing things.

Empathy is important for understanding what it feels like to be part of a minority group. J.B. Phillips put it this way in his translation of Philippians 2:4: "None of you should think only of his own affairs, but each should learn to see things from other peoples' point of view."

One way to learn empathy is to identify some characteristic you have that most people around you do not have. For example, many North Americans are really into the sports. Almost every weekend, a "buffet" of sports shows are available on television—tennis matches, bicycle races, professional baseball games, Olympic games, golf tournaments, track and field meets, basketball games, wrestling, soccer, and more. If you are part of a crowd that loves sports, but you hate sports, how do you think the others would relate to you? How do you think you might feel hanging around a group that always talks about game scores statistics, players' abilities, the quality of sports equipment, and the refereeing?

The experience of feeling like an outsider may cause you to empathize with those who continually face the stigma of being different. It will help you to understand what it feels like to be excluded, powerless to change a situation, or looked down upon. This experience may motivate you to find strategies for including those who are treated negatively because they are different. Kohei Goshi once said, "It may be difficult to teach a person to respect another unless we can help people to see things from the other's point of view."[5]

THREE: LOOSEN UP

A student named Becca shared these fears with her cultural anthropology class: "I want to be friends with people who are ethnically different from me, but I get so nervous. I do not know what to say. In fact, I tend to isolate myself from them because I am afraid that I may say or do something offensive. I do not want to make any mistakes."

There are many people like Becca. They want to reach out to others, but fear holds them back. During a class on intercultural communication at Wheaton College Graduate School, Dr. Lois McKinney gave this simple advice to the class: "Learn to loosen up."

A bit of nervousness usually goes along with meeting new people, whether they are ethnically different from you or not. A little nervousness is not bad; it results from the number of uncertainties that may arise and the risks of becoming involved.

Like Becca, many people avoid cross-cultural contacts because they do not want to make mistakes. But mistakes are bound to happen, no matter how carefully an individual behaves. Building relationships with others involves saying and doing things that may be misinterpreted. While some mistakes may be embarrassing, painful, or even silly, few are likely to be catastrophic. And most can be mended.

FOUR: KEEP YOUR SENSE OF HUMOR

Those who actively develop cross-cultural relationships know that a sense of humor is one of the most important ingredients in creating successful interaction. Be willing to laugh at yourself and with others.

Jun and Mamel are Filipino missionaries who were in the States for a few months to speak about their ministry in Cambodia. They visited a national park in South Dakota where different styles of tepees were on display. One tourist who was taking pictures saw Jun and Mamel. He rushed over and asked if he could take a picture of them standing in front of one of the tepees. The man told Jun and Mamel that he was excited because he had been hoping to get a picture of an authentic Native American house with real Native Americans standing in front of it. The man then asked Jun where he was from.

Jun replied, "From the Philippines."

The man scratched his head and mumbled to his wife that he had never heard of a Native American tribe called the Philippines. He then proceeded to ask Jun and Mamel to fold their arms and look stern while he took their picture.

Were Jun and Mamel offended? Not at all. In fact, Jun shared, "Mamel and I laughed about it afterward. We thought it was funny that we were identified as Native Americans. We chalked it up as one of those 'cute' things Americans do. That man probably has framed our picture and is telling everyone about his contact with real Native Americans."

FIVE: DON'T BE AFRAID OF MISTAKES

Most people are willing to forgive. Samuel wanted his friend Jeff to meet O'Dongo, his college roommate from Africa. After they were introduced, Jeff decided that he wanted to get to know O'Dongo better. Jeff started out by saying, "O'Dongo, it must really be different for you to be living in America. I am sure that you are finding it much easier to have electricity and running water in your dorm. Life must have been very hard for you back in Africa, living in a mud hut with a thatched roof."

O'Dongo replied, "I am sorry, but I have never lived in a mud hut. My house in Africa is very modern. It has electricity and running water just like the houses here in America do."

Jeff was embarrassed. However, instead of shutting himself off from O'Dongo, he humbly asked for forgiveness. In the following weeks, the relationship between Jeff and O'Dongo continued to grow. They became good friends. Jeff said, "I knew I had made a mistake, but I was not going to allow my mistake to mess up the blessing of getting to know O'Dongo. When I asked him to forgive me, he graciously did. Some day I hope to minister in Africa. O'Dongo has been teaching me many things about his homeland. I really enjoy his friendship."

SIX: DO NOT MAKE QUICK JUDGMENTS

In any cross-cultural relationship, one will see and hear new things. Some will seem foreign and strange. In fact, some may even seem bad. It is important to refrain from making judgments too quickly. Peter Elbow says that people should put aside critical thinking until they have had an opportunity to see the other person's viewpoint. This requires careful listening and patience.[6]

Some Cambodians wear gold rings on each of their fingers, numerous gold necklaces around their necks, an array of bracelets around their wrists, and ruby earrings. Even many Christians in Cambodia wear a lot of jewelry. In my early ministry there, I was disturbed by this overt display of wealth. My judgment was based on the teaching I had heard when I was a new convert that "real Christians" do not wear a lot of jewelry.

I began to articulate my feelings to the Cambodian Christians. I believed wearing all this jewelry represented worldliness and carnality. At first no one responded to me. A few months later, however, when they had probably heard enough of my criticism, one of them approached me. What he told me completely changed my perception.

For many years Cambodians had put their money into bank accounts where, they were told, it would be safe. But in the mid-1970s the Khmer Rouge, a communistic group, invaded the land. Their invasion destroyed the security that Cambodians had experienced for many years. Millions were killed. Anything that reflected Western influence was destroyed. Eyeglasses were shattered. Cars were burned. Books were torn to pieces. Banks were set ablaze, and people's life savings went up in smoke. Those who were fortunate enough to escape death by the hands of the Khmer Rouge were left without any earthy security. They were penniless.

Years later, after the Khmer Rouge was forced into the hills near the border with Thailand, banks again began to appear in the cities and towns of Cambodia. But many Cambodians had lost faith in them. The Khmer Rouge's destruction of the banks was evidence to these people that banks were not completely secure. So instead of putting their money into "untrustworthy" bank accounts, they began to use it to buy valuable jewelry.

If history repeats itself and another group like the Khmer Rouge invades Cambodia, many Cambodians assert that they will not be left penniless. They will flee with their jewelry. After this explanation, I began to see the Cambodians' practice of wearing jewelry in a completely different light.

SEVEN: BE TOLERANT OF AMBIGUITY

In order to create effective cross-cultural relationships, one must be tolerant of ambiguity. People who cannot tolerate ambiguity are those who insist upon precise, clearly defined expectations. Going outside the boundaries would be unacceptable in their minds.

Ambiguous situations are bound to arise as we relate to those from other cultural backgrounds. During such times, one should display as little discomfort as possible. Showing too much discomfort—such as confusion, frustration, or even hostility—may cause others to become displeased.

Dave and his family were invited to attend an African-American church. With great enthusiasm Dave accepted the invitation. He saw this as a wonderful opportunity to see how another group of Christians worshiped. He was told that the church service began at 10:00 A.M. To ensure that they would find seats, Dave and his family arrived at 9:45.

Sam, the friend who had extended the invitation, met Dave and his family at the entrance of the church. After being ushered in, they sat down and waited for the service to begin. Dave's friend hung around for a while and then excused himself to talk to someone else. At ten o'clock nothing was taking place on the platform. The lights were still dim, and the members of the congregation were milling around, talking and laughing with each other. Dave and his family sat patiently. Members of the church frequently stopped by and introduced themselves, telling Dave's family how glad they were that they had come to worship with them. Sam also came by often to see how they were doing. At 10:15 there was still nothing happening on the platform. Dave and his family continued to wait patiently. The worship service finally started at 10:45.

The worship services that Dave usually attended typically lasted for about one hour and fifteen minutes. When he accepted the invitation, Dave assumed the service there would last about the same length of time. However, one hour after the service started, people were still singing hymns and choruses. It was one hour and twenty minutes before the pastor finally stood to preach. The sermon then lasted for another hour. When the preaching came to an end, a long altar service followed. After the altar service, those who had made decisions were encouraged to give testimonies, telling the congregation what God had done for them.

As Dave and his family learned, those who attended this church placed great value on Christian fellowship. To their way of thinking, fellowship with other believers was an important part of worship. Although Dave found himself in a culturally ambiguous situation, he did not allow his preconceived ideas about the form and timing of worship to sabotage a wonderful opportunity for cross-cultural interaction.

EIGHT: DEVELOP INTERCULTURAL TRAITS

After working in several countries with people from diverse backgrounds, I have discovered that certain traits can help a person be more successful in encounters with those from different ethnic backgrounds. I suggest the following.

Curiosity

Curiosity has a way of drawing people beyond familiar boundaries. In fact, attempting to understand other people and why they behave as they do can help override your own anxieties, shyness, and insecurities.

My brother Tom lives in Brooklyn, New York. He successfully relates to people from many different backgrounds. When I am with him, I notice that he continually asks people questions. Then he sincerely listens to what they have to say. His curiosity enables him to learn about other people and their lifestyles.

Courage

Janelle shared that one of the hardest things for her to do is to meet new people. As she put it, "Fear freezes me from stepping out."

Years ago, I was part of a church that decided to survey its members to discover how friendly the church was to visitors. Two of the questions they asked were: (1) Do you approach visitors to introduce yourself and get to know them? and, (2) If you answered "no," what is the reason you do not?

The predominant answer to the first question was "no." The predominant answer to the second question was "fear." It takes a certain amount of courage to meet people.

Friendliness

I recall exiting church one Sunday and remarking to my wife that the people there were some of the most unfriendly around. Roxy then asked me a very pointed question: "Jim, are you friendly to them?"

Throughout the week I thought about her question. My reflections revealed that I usually went to church, sat down, opened my bulletin and buried my nose in it. The truth was that I was not being friendly. Although I was in the midst of a crowded church, I had put up an invisible barrier that announced to others, "Leave me alone!"

The next Sunday I decided to do things differently. I did not bury my nose in my bulletin. Instead, I made an effort to talk to those around me. After church I commented to Roxy, "Wow! We have a warm and friendly church."

With a twinkle in her eye, Roxy said, "He who wants friends must show himself friendly."

Flexibility

To be flexible is to be adaptable. In other words, flexibility is the ability to make basic changes in thinking. It is a willingness to experience new ways of feeling and to consider new ways of doing. The opposite of being flexible is being rigid—unwilling to change, even if the situation calls for change.

Communication

For several years I have taught students how to evangelize. I asked one class what prevented them from sharing their faith with others. Fear was the top reason on their list, but I was more intrigued by the second reason they gave. It was that they did not know how to start a conversation with another person.

I've heard that people like to talk about themselves. There is a lot of truth behind that statement. One way to start a conversation is to find out what interests the other person, then get him or her to talk about it.

When my family and I returned to America from Zimbabwe after four years of missionary service, we spent a few days in New York City with my brother Tom. While we were there, we decided to visit the Statue of Liberty by way of a ferry. As the boat glided along the gentle rippling water, I overheard someone say *mvura*.

I had used the word *mvura* in Africa. In the Shona language it means water. All I could think was, "I must have heard wrong. This is America and not Zimbabwe."

However, a few moments later the gentleman next to me again used the word *mvura*.

My curiosity was piqued. Mustering all the courage I could, I turned to the man and asked, "Did you just use the word *mvura*?"

"Yes, I did. Why do you ask?"

"I worked in Africa for four years, and the Shona who attended the church I started used the word *mvura*."

That opened the gate. The man was a Zimbabwean who was living in New York. As we engaged in conversation, we discovered that we had mutual friends who were living in Bulawayo, Zimbabwe (what a small world!). By the time the ferry ride came to an end, I felt as if I had made a friend. As we walked down the gangplank, the man said to me, "Thank you for giving me your ear. It has been so good to talk about my country to someone who has actually been there."

NINE: TAKE A STAND

Ethnic jokes usually ridicule the "out" group while enhancing the teller's "in" group. Ethnic joking is derisive and demeaning to persons and groups. Seeing things from the differing perspective of the "out" group may open your eyes to what is really happening when people tell ethnic jokes or make other kinds of derisive comments. Let's look at some examples from both sides.

Part of the "in" Group

Greg was invited by some of his friends to go to the mall. While they were walking around, one of the guys began making derogatory statements about different races. Before long he was using unkind names to identify them. When he realized that he was getting a big laugh from his buddies, he used even more offensive names to identify other groups.

Some of Marie's friends like to tell ethnic jokes. They defend their actions saying that their joking doesn't really hurt anybody—that ethnic jokes are just another form of humor.

Part of the "out" Group

Let's hear a different perspective from two minority group members.

Eric. "My name is Eric. I am from South America. Most of the people with whom I hang out are white Americans. Part of the reason that this is true is because there are not many South Americans living in my community. Since I am short and very dark, I usually stick out in a crowd.

"Those I hang around with sometimes tell jokes or say things at my expense. The other day one of them said to me, 'All you South Americans are the same. You come here and mooch off of us.'

"That really hurt my feelings. I wanted to say something, but I decided that I would just keep my mouth shut."

Carmen. "I'm Carmen and I am Native American. I decided to attend a university which had a student body predominantly made up of middle-class white students. While I was there, I heard many students say things like, 'Indians are lazy'; 'they are all on welfare'; 'those redskins are only good for drinking and getting drunk.' When they caught themselves saying these things in my presence, they would say things like, 'Carmen, you know we weren't referring to you—you are different from the rest of them' or 'We were only joking, Carmen; we didn't mean any harm by what we said.' After the first semester I quit and went home."

Learn from Failure

As Christians we should ask God to give us the courage to speak up on behalf of ethnic groups when unjust statements are made about them. There is a place for Christians to take a stand on behalf of those who are being unfairly picked on.

This incident from my missionary career does not make me proud at all. On one occasion I was traveling to a village in South Africa to coordinate and teach some pastors' seminars. Since my destination was so far away, I had to make several stops at cafés to stretch my legs and eat. At one café I noticed a big commotion taking place. As I neared the entrance, I saw a white teenager using a shambock (a type of rubber whip) to hit the back of an old black man. I felt very uneasy as I saw what was happening. I felt I should step up and stop it. However, all I could think was, "Jim, this is none of your affair. Buy what you must and move on."

That is exactly what I did. As I drove down the road, I felt horrible. The question that kept running through my mind was, "What would Jesus Christ have done?" I think He would have grabbed the shambock out of the hand of the teenager to stop the degrading beating of the old man. To this day, I remember the incident with discomfort and shame. I should have taken a stand to defend the weak and defenseless.

Be Strong and Brave

My sons, André and Matthew, taught me a valuable lesson about taking a stand. When we first arrived in South Africa, some places still had separate restrooms for Whites and Blacks.

While we were at a shopping center, my boys (who were probably around ten years old at the time) said they needed to use the restroom. We quickly located restrooms, only to be confronted by a choice. Since we were of Chinese descent, we were considered Whites and could have used the restroom labeled "for Whites only." My boys, however, would not use it. They walked straight to the Blacks' restroom with many people staring at them.

When I asked them why they decided to use the Blacks' restroom, they answered, "Because we want to make a point. We are taking a stand. You preached that Christians sometimes need to be strong and brave. We are just doing what you taught us."

TEN: RECOGNIZE THAT WE DO NOT LIVE IN A COLORLESS OR CULTURELESS WORLD

I heard someone suggest that we should seek to live in a colorless and cultureless world as the means of eliminating racial tensions. In other words, he advocated a world where everyone would basically be the same, allowing all people to live in peace with each other. When asked what I thought about this suggestion, I replied, "I like it a lot, as long as everyone is just like me. What a wonderful world this would be if everyone looked like me, thought liked me, talked like me, and behaved like me."

I can almost hear you groaning as you answer, "How boring!" You would be right. Life would be boring if we were all alike. Besides, this is not how God created us.

God's Artistic Palette

Consider the issue of color. Could we ever really live in a colorless world? The answer is no. To even try would be unrealistic, since God *did* create color. Further, I believe He made color for us to enjoy.

I derive joy from watching sunsets. The mixture of a sunset's colors is amazing to me. Though I do not have a green thumb, I love looking at flowers. There is glorious beauty in their variety of colors. I also take pleasure in watching trees change colors during the fall. The bright yellows, purples, and reds make me want to praise the Great Creator.

Can you remember when there was only black-and-white television? I can. As a child I remember watching many good black-and-white TV programs. I was content watching them—until I saw my first color television set. Mesmerized, I sat watching Rocky and Bullwinkle, Gumby, and Underdog in living color. Would I ever go back to watching a black-and-white television? Perhaps if I had to, but I have been spoiled. Give me color any day! I like color, and I praise God that He allows me to be surrounded by it.

Ivan Beals wrote, "We must neither deny color nor idolize it with pride."[7] We cannot dismiss it since God did make each one of us with color. Whether or not we want to admit it, color is a tangible factor of personhood. Color is part of a person's total being. The problem is not that we are creatures of color. The problem is that we judge others according to their color.

It is sad when the world pressures people into judging their own color as bad. I ministered in South Africa during the final years of apartheid, when many Blacks were dissatisfied with their skin color. They wanted to be white, since Whites were given advantages that they were not given. Because of this dissatisfaction, pharmaceutical companies developed creams that were supposed to lighten a person's skin color. Many Blacks bought the creams and began applying them to their flesh. The problem was that some of the creams had not been properly tested and were unsafe to use. Instead of lightening people's skin evenly, they lightened some parts and darkened others, causing the users to be permanently blotched.

It's Nonnegotiable

It's ironic that in some cultures people want to be lighter, while in other cultures people want to be darker. In Cambodia, pregnant women eat apples because they believe this will make their babies whiter. On the other hand, many Americans visit tanning salons or subject themselves to large doses of sunlight in order to darken their skin.

The color with which we were born is a nonnegotiable. For this reason I do not believe that one should ever be made to feel shame or feel the need to apologize for his or her skin color. As Christians we should never make others feel inferior because of their skin color. God made us with color. We should enjoy and appreciate His artistic touch in the lives of all His creatures. Our differences have a way of making life interesting.

CASE STUDY: STAN'S DILEMMA

Stan is traveling in a van. Those who are in the van with Stan seem to know each other fairly well. They are joking and laughing with each other. Since Stan is new to the group, he spends more time watching and listening than joining in and talking. After a while, the talking turns to ethnic joking. Stan feels uncomfortable with the comments that are being made.

What are Stan's options in this situation?

To think about . . .

1. To what primary groups did you belong when you were young? How did the primary group with which you were identified influence the way you think and do things today?
2. What are your primary group associations now, and how do these groups influence your thoughts and behavior?
3. Describe a time when you were not part of the "in" group. How did you feel when you were excluded? What might someone from the "in" group have done to make you feel part of the group? What might you do to make a person who is different feel welcome in your group?
4. How would you have reacted if you were Jun or Mamel and had been asked to pose in front of a tepee because you were mistaken for a Native American?
5. Have you ever made a serious blunder (like Jim with O'Dongo) when trying to be friendly to someone of another culture? How did you react when you realized your mistake? How did the other person respond?
6. What might have happened if Dave and his family had left church after an hour instead of staying through the entire service?
7. Have you ever taken a stand to defend someone who was the target of racial prejudice or confronted someone who was disparaging an ethnic group? Describe your experience.

Chapter Seven

How the Church Can Help

> Go to the people
>> Live among them
>> Learn from them
>> Love them
> Start with what they know
>> Build on what they have:
> But of the best leaders
>> When their task is accomplished
>> Their work is done
> The people will remark
>> "We have done it ourselves."
>
> —Chinese poem

For the past several years, I have taken students to Chicago for spring break. During the week I try to expose them to different cultures and ministries. This year my students came face-to-face with Chinese, Thai, Bosnians, Hispanics, Koreans, Africans, and African Americans. At the end of the week, I allowed time for the students to share their thoughts and feelings. Here are some of their responses:

"I dreaded coming on this trip but I knew that God wanted me to. I was not sure how I was going to relate to people from different ethnic backgrounds. But I am so glad that I did come. I have learned so much. People are people no matter where you go."

"We went to a Bosnian home. They were refugees. I never thought it possible, but even though I could not speak their language and they could not speak English, we were still able to connect with each other. It was such a wonderful experience drinking coffee and eating cookies with them."

"I have always gone to a church which was all White. I knew there were people of different colors out there, but I never thought much about them. I was comfortable in my church. In fact, I heard some in my church say that it is unbiblical for there to be multi-ethnic churches. Their reason is that God made our differences to keep us separate from each other. They are so wrong."

"The Church can be such a powerful change agent. Churches should be helping their members appreciate diversity, instead of being scared of it."

The words "the Church can be such a powerful change agent" keep ringing in my ears. This is so true. The Church cannot close its eyes and act as if diversity is not a Church issue. People from all walks of life are moving next door to us.

I recently heard about an apartment building in Fort Wayne, Indiana, in which fifteen different languages are spoken. Churches really must help their members appreciate diversity, instead of fearing and avoiding it. So, how can a church help its members appreciate cultural diversity? Each church has a distinct personality, but the following twelve guidelines will be useful in a variety of situations.

ONE: OBEY GOD AND GO

Twenty-six years ago, Wayne Gordon was a college graduate who had a deep burden to be the type of Christian that God wanted him to be. A young, all-American kind of guy from Iowa, Wayne sensed that God wanted him to go to Chicago to minister to young people. After much prayer and soul searching, Wayne headed for the Windy City to make a difference in the lives of inner city youth.

An Incarnational Lifestyle

Wayne moved to North Lawndale, a residential area of Chicago that most white Christians avoided. His friends tried to talk him out of this decision, telling him that he was asking for trouble. They said it was insane for a white man to move into a predominantly African-American neighborhood. The only other ethnic groups in that area were a small number of Hispanics and Asians.

However, Wayne's friends and their words of impending doom did not deter him. He moved in and became the only White in North Lawndale. He soon started a Bible study with the young athletes he was coaching. People expected his inner-city ministry to be short lived. But Wayne stayed and made Lawndale his home. He married Anne and raised his children there. Why did he stay? According to John Perkins it was "because of his competitive nature, his enormous heart, and his inexhaustible drive, and partly because he never thought of failure [that] Wayne chose to live among, and then identify with, the people he wanted to reach with the good news of Jesus Christ."[1]

For more than twenty years Wayne has remained in the inner city, choosing an incarnational lifestyle. His neighbors' felt needs became his felt needs. What began as a small Bible study has developed into Lawndale Community Church which presently has a staff of 150. It has been instrumental in helping more than fifty young people enter and graduate from colleges or universities, and it runs a clinic that treats fifty thousand patients annually.

What began as a vision has become a reality because a young man from Iowa was willing to obey God—and *go!* Today, North Lawndale is no longer the battered community Wayne first walked into years ago. God has been using people of all colors, socioeconomic backgrounds, and ages to transform a once dilapidated community into a place where love is demonstrated in practical and miraculous ways.

An International Church

Donovan Shoemaker, who calls himself "a transplanted Indiana farm boy," became the pastor of First Wesleyan Church in Jersey City, New Jersey, twenty-nine years ago. When he and his wife, Viola, first arrived, the neighborhood around the church was changing and the church was declining. Reflecting on those early days, Pastor Shoemaker commented, "The church was about half white and half black, but it was still very much under the control of the older members, most of whom were white. The black members sort of sat back and let the white members lead things."

Today, First Wesleyan Church in Jersey City is thriving. Instead of moving to a different location when the community began to change in "color," the pastor and leaders of the church decided to stay. Sixty percent of those who now attend the church are immigrants or their children. Flags representing more than forty different nations hang around the sanctuary. Donovan and Viola Shoemaker appreciate diversity. They are making a difference in Jersey City because they were and are willing to be used by God. They were willing to go!

Both Wayne Gordon and Donovan Shoemaker have been obedient to the Great Commission. Matthew 28:18–19 makes it clear that while disciples of Christ should be concerned about cultivating their spiritual lives, they also need to be concerned about reaching out to others in need. The great missiologist Herbert Kane contends that there must come a time when the disciple becomes an apostle, going forth to others with the saving gospel of Jesus Christ.

TWO: GET INVOLVED IN LIVES

I have a friend who was involved briefly with an inner-city ministry. The board members articulated a desire to minister to people from different ethnic backgrounds. What they said made my friend very excited. He thought, "This is a ministry I can really sink my teeth into."

After a few board meetings, however, he began to realize that the actions of the board members did not match their words. Very seldom did the members come into contact with the local population. They always held their meetings in a suburban home. When my friend mentioned this to the board, he was told it would be too much "hassle" to move the meetings into the inner-city house that had been purchased for the ministry.

"There is no air conditioning in the house."

"The mosquitoes are horrendous down there."

"We don't want to park our cars down there—someone may break into them."

At another meeting, my friend suggested that the committee consider setting up a basketball hoop on the property of the inner-city house, so that the youth of the neighborhood would have a place to play. Once again he met opposition from the ministry board members.

"If we do that we will have a bunch of kids hanging around our house. They may damage our property!"

"The kind of youth who would play basketball around this place would be the undesirable kinds. Some of them may be drug addicts or drunks—they would be the really bad ones."

"The young people who would be using our hoop would need supervision. We just don't have the time to stand guard over them."

"We can't set up that hoop. Don't you know what happens with nice things in the inner city? They quickly get destroyed. Those kinds of people just do not know how to take care of things."

My friend was stunned by their responses. He thought, "How are we to have an effective ministry to others if we are not willing to get close to them?"

If Christians plan to minister to people from different ethnic backgrounds, they will need to get personally involved in their lives. That is what Jesus Christ did. He associated with people, spending time talking to them, listening to them, walking with them, eating with them, and worshiping with them.

THREE: MINISTER TO PEOPLE, NOT TO NUMBERS

Someone once gave me this insightful advice: Invest in people and not in programs. Think of people who are different from you as *people* and not as *numbers* for church programs.

A group of students and I were involved in a visitation program, a ministry that targeted the inner city. As we walked through the community, we saw an older Hispanic man sitting in a rickety chair on his porch. One student suggested, "Let's go witness to him."

Puffing on his cigar, the old man studied us as we approached, then spoke loudly enough for us to hear: "Here we go again. Another bunch of Christian fanatics trying to win me to Jesus."

Startled by his comment, I said, "Excuse me, what did you say?"

Even louder than before, he replied:

You heard me. I get so tired of you Christians. You come here and tell us that you love us. However, we only see you once and never again. We don't like to be statistics that you can record somewhere. If you really loved me and the people in this area, you wouldn't just visit us once. You would make the effort to visit us regularly and get to know us. Don't think I don't know what you're going to do after you leave. You're going to go back to wherever you are from and report that you talked to this many Blacks, or this many Mexicans, or this many such and such. We don't need that. We're not just numbers. We are people just like you, and we want to be treated like people.

I learned an important lesson that day. In seeking to be cross-culturally sensitive, especially as we minister in the name of Jesus Christ, we must remember that getting personally involved in people's lives means putting faces on our numbers.

FOUR: MINISTER IN HUMILITY

Years ago, Tony Campolo said something that made a big impression on me. He stressed that Christians should avoid ministering to people from a position of power, instead of a position of humility.

Thomas Ehrich put it this way:

We would all find more serenity in life if we could be done with comparisons and envy. God made us diverse, and, in God's eyes at least, our diversity lacks hierarchy. As a friend says in her song *Weave*, God makes of us a "symphony": Different instruments playing in harmony. Each part matters, but only if it's played according to its calling and isn't fighting another part for control. We in the church make better music when we treasure our diversity, rather than stifle it.[2]

I like taking students with me when I minister in different inner cities. When the opportunity arises, I encourage them to ask questions. Asking questions can be a sign of humility. Through their questions and willingness to listen, some students have discovered that many people feel "looked down on" when someone ministers to them.

Joan was very transparent when she shared her thoughts:

I do not mean to do this, but I catch myself treating people of color differently than I do those who are like me. It was ingrained in me as a child that my race was the superior race. When I became a Christian, my eyes were opened up to the fact that this is not true. However, I still catch myself feeling superior to people of color. My tendency is to tell them what to do.

Carmen shared:

As a Native American, I feel offended when I sense I am being talked down to. I realize that Native Americans need help. However, so do Blacks and many Asians and even Whites. I would rather not accept any help if it is going to be demeaning. . . . often times we feel as if people come to minister to us just to make themselves feel good. I do not like it when people have to make us feel bad in order to make themselves feel good. I would rather that people not come to us with their help if they are going to treat us like poor, pitiful Indians. No matter how sad our situation may be, we still want to be treated with dignity.

Remembering that Jesus ministered from a position of humility and not of power is key to ministering effectively. That's a lesson that should be applied not only to cross-cultural interaction, but to all areas of Christian ministry.

FIVE: RETHINK THE HOMOGENEOUS CHURCH

For many years church growth leaders have stressed homogeneity as the fast track to "growing the church." While it is true that homogeneous churches have been easier to grow, Christians should not take the easiest path, but the biblical path. Sadly, some pastors have used the concept of homogeneity to justify segregated congregations.

Raleigh Washington declared, "Homogeneous churches may be easier, but I don't think they are God's intent. The first New Testament church at Antioch had elders who were from different races and cultures. That's our model church. When we get to heaven, it's not going to be homogeneous. Where better to start than right here?"[3]

In rethinking the concept of the homogeneous church, we would do well to study this 1973 position statement of the Christian Holiness Association (known today as Christian Holiness Partnership):

> The Bible indicates the church is the community of Christ on earth, model of loving, caring . . . human relationships and a loving, obedient relationship to God in Christ. The world will listen to our pronouncements on racism, poverty and morality when we demonstrate to them what life can be when Christ's tenets are followed. For Christ compressed all that matters most into one word, LOVE—Love to God and Love to Man. That word demonstrated in Christ's cross put an end to artificial, separating, sinful barriers in human relations.[4]

SIX: UNDERSTAND FIRST, SECOND, AND THIRD GENERATIONS

Churches that plan to minister to those who are ethnically different must understand the differences between the first, second, and third generations.

How the First Generation Sees It

My mother was the first person in her family to come to America from China. After arriving in America, she held on to many of her Chinese ways. She felt comfortable wearing traditional Chinese clothing, eating Chinese food, and filling her house with Chinese ornaments and furniture. Most of her new friends were Chinese who had also recently come to America. Though she was now physically living in America, she was still psychologically living in China.

Many first-generation immigrants are like my mother. They recognize that they live in America, but they cling onto the old ways of doing things. This is one reason why places like New York City's Chinatown and German Town, or Chicago's Little Italy are so popular. Upon entering one of these ethnic enclaves, people feel as if they have entered a foreign country. While visiting Chinatown, some of my university students made such comments as, "It's as if I am in China," "Everyone speaks Chinese," "All the signs are written in Chinese characters," "This place smells like I would expect China to smell."

How the Second Generation Sees It

While first-generation immigrants tend to hold on to their ethnic backgrounds, their children, who have been born in America, tend to feel uncomfortable with their ethnicity. I was born in America. When I entered my early teens, I felt embarrassed about being Chinese. During this period of my life, I began to reject almost everything that was Chinese or hinted at being from China. (The only thing I wanted to hold on to was Chinese food—the food of heaven!) No longer did I want to speak Chinese. Since I was an American, I was going to speak English. In fact, my attitude caused me to avoid other Orientals. I saw them as being provincial, backward, and unsophisticated. This created tension among my family members. Since they were Chinese, I even felt embarrassed being with them. All my friends were either Whites or African-Americans.

How the Third Generation Sees It

While the second generation may feel uncomfortable about its racial background, third-generation immigrants are more comfortable with their roots. Many of them do research to understand the history of their ancestors and their culture. Many third-generation Americans also learn to speak the language of their relatives. In other words, they are more comfortable in two or more cultures. They have no problem being a part of both the American culture and the culture of their ancestors.

How this Relates to the Church

You may be wondering, "How does this relate to the ministry of the Church?" The characteristics of first, second, and third generation immigrants readily translate into the Church's experience of cross-cultural interaction.

First-generation immigrants often do not want to be integrated into American churches. They may visit an English-speaking church out of courtesy. But they would rather start their own worship services where they can speak their native languages and be around others from their own cultural background. One way an established American church can minister to this generation is to allow them to use the sanctuary at a time when the English-speaking congregation is not using it. That will allow the new group to worship in its own language and in the style to which it is accustomed.

Many of the second generation do not feel comfortable worshiping in services that reflect the culture of their ancestors. Because they do not see themselves as part of their parents' culture, they often feel lonely and ignored. They want to be seen as fully American and are more open to attending an English-speaking service. When they do attend, they do not want members of the congregation to highlight the fact that they are different.

If the church will reach out to second-generation immigrants, it will see wonderful results. By showing a little attention to this group, making them feel welcome, and seeking to fellowship with them, the church may see many new converts.

I have often heard teachers of evangelism tell their students that before they talk about the church they should talk about Jesus Christ. The idea is to get people saved first so that they will want to come to the church. This is not necessarily true with non-Christian second-generation Americans. In fact, the opposite is true. Members of the second generation need to feel welcomed and accepted first. If they can be made to feel comfortable within the body of Christ, there is a greater chance that they will listen to what Christians have to say about Christ. Their first need is to feel loved, cared about, and included.

Those in the third generation feel comfortable having their feet in two cultures. But even though they view themselves as bicultural, when they attend church they want to be treated like Americans. It is not that they are uncomfortable with their ethnic heritage; they just do not want this difference to be highlighted. As an example, third-generation Chinese Americans have shared how annoying it is when people in the church say to them, "You're Chinese. When did you come to this country?" or, "What Chinese foods do you eat in your home?" It is not that they are ashamed of being Chinese, nor that they do not want to talk about their Chinese heritage. They simply want to be recognized as being Americans as well.

	First Generation	**Second Generation**	**Third Generation**
Mind-Set	I am still part of my "home" culture.	I am an American.	I am an American, but I am interested in my roots.
Attitudes	My home culture is the best. The culture of America is bad.	The culture of my parents is bad. The culture of America is good.	The culture of my roots needs to be investigated. The culture of America has good and bad elements.
Find Comfort	I find comfort being with others who strongly identify with my home culture.	I find comfort being with those who identify with American culture.	I find comfort being in the American culture, and in my root culture.
Find Discomfort	I feel uncomfortable when I am not with those who are part of my home culture.	I feel uncomfortable when I am not included by Americans.	I feel uncomfortable when I am identified only by my root culture and not as an American also.

SEVEN: PROVIDE RESOURCES

Christians are continually exposed to different forms of media: television, movies, books, audiotapes, videotapes, music, newspapers, magazines, and the Internet, to name a few. Each of these can influence a person's attitudes, beliefs, and behaviors positively or negatively. Lawndale Community Church in Chicago built a library a few years ago to house books, magazines, audiotapes, and videotapes that deal with the issues of ethnicity and how the church can minister in a context of diversity.[5] A church might consider establishing a section in its church library for resources that deal with issues of diversity. Using various forms of media is an excellent way to combat and reduce prejudice.

EIGHT: EDUCATE

Churches should also educate people on diversity issues. I know of one church that used its Sunday school hour for three months to teach about cultural diversity.

Before sending short-term mission teams, some churches train team members to better relate to those from different cultures. One church used children's sermons to educate its young children about the need to be culturally sensitive. Other churches have developed home fellowship groups in which the participants are given the opportunity to discuss the theology of diversity.

NINE: USE MISSIONARIES AS RESOURCES

Some churches use missions conferences to teach about other cultures and how to reach out to them. Missionaries are wonderful resources for teaching cross-cultural interaction, but many churches do not make the most of them. Too often, missionaries are given time for a sermon only, or just a few five- to ten-minute spots over an entire weekend.

As a missionary I really appreciated churches that put me to work when I visited them. One church I attended asked me to speak several times during the two days I was with them. On Saturday I spoke at a men's breakfast, a missions training seminar, a ladies' luncheon, a small group fellowship, and a teen afterglow. On Sunday I preached in the early worship hour, taught the adult Sunday school class, spoke to a children's Sunday school class, and preached at the second worship service. The theme of my teaching and preaching was "Reaching Those in Jerusalem, Judea, Samaria, and the Uttermost Parts of the World." The missions committee had asked me to tell how each person who attended the church could touch those around him—especially those who were ethnically different. They wanted the members of the church to recognize that missions doesn't take place only overseas. America is a mission field too.

TEN: PARTICIPATE IN DIFFERENT STYLES OF WORSHIP

I enjoy visiting ethnically different churches. My experiences in these churches continually remind me that the God I serve is creative. They remind me that God, in His goodness, allows for many different ways of worshiping Him. Just as important, I like being reminded that I am part of a great big family, made up of people from all walks of life.

As a professor of intercultural studies, I require my students to attend churches that are ethnically different. I want them to experience the creativity of God for themselves. To this day I have not had one student tell me that the experience was negative. I have asked them, "Should I strike this requirement from the syllabus?" I have always been emphatically told, "No!"

This does not mean that the experience is always comfortable for them. They frequently report being out of their comfort zones when visiting ethnic churches. The majority of the students report at least some frustration and feelings of confusion when worshiping in styles to which they are unaccustomed. However, they also share that the experience stretches them to think in a "bigger" way.

ELEVEN: EXCHANGE LEADERS

Some churches swap pastors occasionally. One church in Chicago regularly invites ethnic pastors or worship teams to lead their worship services. I also saw this done effectively in South Africa. Black pastors were invited to speak from pulpits ordinarily occupied by Whites, and visa versa. This is an excellent way to broaden cross-cultural perspectives.

TWELVE: HOLD COMMUNITY WORSHIP SERVICES

A church in San Antonio, Texas, used to host community singspirations. Churches of various denominations were invited to participate. At each singspiration, a different church was invited to lead the service. Since San Antonio is such a multicultural city, it has many ethnically diverse churches. Hearing praises to God in English, Spanish, Chinese, and Korean was both enjoyable and inspiring. Those attending also felt a warm sense of camaraderie. Differences were not accented. Instead, the services stressed oneness in Christ. Even though the participants were from many different cultures, in Christ they really were one.

THE RAINBOW TEAM

I arose early one Saturday several years ago to take my daily jog. The sun was quickly warming South Africa's cool night air. As I began to run, I noticed other runners. It was unusual to see so many of them out that early.

"Hey, what's up?" I asked one of them.

"We're running to the starting line. There is a thirty-kilometer race today."

I had been running on a regular basis for several months. When opportunity allowed, I would enter races. Being with other runners has a way of pumping me up. I had already participated in ten-, fifteen-, and twenty-kilometer races, but never a thirty-kilometer race. Thirty kilometers is about 18.75 miles. In less than a second, I made up my mind that I was going to enter the race. I ran home, got money to pay the entrance fee, ran back to the starting line, and waited for the gun to go off. As I stood there, my body tensed with anticipation. I especially enjoy the start of races. The adrenaline was flowing through every vein in my body!

When the gun went off, I felt as if I began to float along in a sea of runners. For the first ten kilometers, I was relaxed. It felt good to be moving. The course at first did not seem too difficult. The road we were running had gentle, rolling hills. However, by the fifteen–kilometer mark the terrain changed drastically. The gentle hills were replaced by what seemed like steep, monstrous mountains. My legs ached with each step. By the twenty-five–kilometer mark,

I wanted to give up. It was a struggle just to get my legs to move. I began making many rest stops to catch my breath. By the twenty-eight–kilometer mark, I was a virtual zombie. Sitting down on one of the curbs, I decided to wait for a car to pick me up and drive me to the finish line. My race was over.

As I sat there feeling dejected and defeated, three runners ran up to me. One of them said, "Hey, man, get up! Don't give up! You're too close to the finish line to give up now! We'll run with you. You can do it!"

I struggled to my feet. Two others took my arms to help me.

"Listen, man, you go the pace you want," another one said. "We'll follow your pace. We're not going to leave you until we cross the line together."

We all ran side by side for two kilometers. They cracked jokes. They asked me questions about why I was in Africa, about my family, and about my running. The conversation directed my focus away from my aching body. Before I knew it, we were entering the stadium.

"You did it! Only one more lap around the track and we're done."

New energy surged through my body. The crowd encouraged us. As we approached the finish line, we could hear the announcer speaking over the public address system, "Look at the group that is coming in now. They represent the new South Africa. Look at them run. What a team they are. Let's cheer for The Rainbow Team!"

Rainbow team? What did he mean? As I glanced at the other three runners in my group, I suddenly understood. The group was composed of a Black, an Indian, a Caucasian, and a Chinese. I had not noticed that while we were running. I just saw them as fellow runners who had helped a fallen runner. However, the announcer was right. We truly were a rainbow team!

As Christian, that's great way to look at our participation in the wondrous diversity of the human race! Can we, through cross-cultural interaction, begin to see ourselves not as black or white or yellow or red, but as fellow runners helping one another finish the race to which God has called us?

Jesus looked at them and said, "With man this is impossible, but not with God; all things are possible with God."

—Mark 10:27

CASE STUDY: BURDENED FOR PEOPLE

While a student at Indiana Wesleyan University, Adam Lipscomb's heart became burdened for people who lived in the inner city of Marion, Indiana. After much prayer, Adam asked for and was given permission to move off campus. He rented an apartment in the center of the inner city. Before long his house was a hub of activity. Children of all colors constantly visited him. Teenagers sought him out to talk. A highlight of his time in the inner city was putting together a community block party. People of all ages and ethnic backgrounds enjoyed playing games and eating with one another.

Why do you think Adam was so effective in touching the lives of inner-city people?

To think about . . .

1. List ways your church can become a "change agent" in your neighborhood. Where do you think your church might start?
2. Can you think of a situation in which a church group's words about change did not match its actions? Where else in society does this happen?
3. How can a church grow numerically but still keep an emphasis on personal interaction?
4. Share a time when you looked down on someone, even though you didn't mean to. How did you rectify the situation? What lessons did you learn?
5. Have you noticed a difference in how various generations respond in a worship setting? List some of the differences in their expectations? How does your church deal with generational differences?
6. Do you think your church would be willing to participate in a pulpit exchange or community worship service? Why or why not?

Afterword

I praise the Lord for what He is doing in my own denomination, The Wesleyan Church. More than twenty-five years ago I made the decision that I wanted to serve the Lord within this denomination, primarily because of its emphasis on salvation and sanctification.

Over the years I have seen the church make great strides in ministering to different racial groups. On a personal level, I am feeling more accepted and appreciated than ever before. Although the church I attend is predominately white, I have felt loved and welcomed by its members, and our pastor does a wonderful job of promoting diversity in the church. The congregation can sense his passionate desire to reach as many people as possible with the message of God's love and salvation, regardless of their ethnic background, skin color, or language.

I have discovered that a person who truly is filled with God's holiness will become a person who loves all people, no matter how different they may be. I have seen this truth become reality all over the world.

It is my prayer that Christians in North America will become so filled with the love of God that they will reach out to those around them from different ethnic backgrounds. May God grant you the courage to move out of your comfort zone and intentionally create relationships with those who are different.

NOTES

Introduction

1. Marlin Mull, "God's Kingdom Includes Everyone," in *Cross-Cultural Church Planting* (Indianapolis: General Department of Evangelism and Church Growth, The Wesleyan Church, 1999), 22.

2. David Hesselgrave, "Ten Major Trends in World Missions," *World Evangelization* (May/June 1988): 14.

3. Ibid.

Chapter 1: The World Is Shrinking!

1. C. Kuckkohn and H. A. Murray, *Personality in Nature, Culture and Society* (New York: Alfred A. Knopf, 1956), 226.

2. *Time* (July 8, 1985).

Chapter 3: Appreciating Diversity

1. Duane Elmer, *Cross-Cultural Conflict: Building Relationships for Effective Ministry* (Downers Grove, Ill.: InterVarsity Press, 1993), 24.

2. W. Ralph Thompson, "Last Things in God's Redemptive Plan," in *A Contemporary Wesleyan Theology,* ed. Charles Carter (Grand Rapids: Zondervan Publishing House, 1983), 1131.

3. William Barclay, *The Gospel of Matthew,* vol. 1 (Philadelphia: Westminster Press, 1975), 17.

4. Adam Clarke, *The New Testament of Our Lord and Saviour Jesus Christ,* vol. 1 (New York: Methodist Book Concern, n.d.), 761.

5. Charles Carter, Acts, *The Wesleyan Bible Commentary* (Grand Rapids: Baker Book House, 1966), 546.

6. Reuben H. Brooks, "Cross-Cultural Perspectives in Christian Education" in *Foundations of Ministry: An Introduction to Christian Education for a New Generation,* ed. Michael J. Anthony (Wheaton, Ill.: Victor/BridgePoint Books, 1992), 107–8.

Chapter 4: Barriers to Building Cross-Cultural Relationships

1. W. G. Sumner, *Folkways: A Study of the Sociological Importance of Usages, Manners, Customers, Mores and Morals* (New York: Dover Publishing, 1906), 11.

2. W. B. Gudykunst and Y. Y. Kim, *Communicating with Strangers* (Reading, PA: Addison-Wesley Educational Publishing, 1984), 142.

3. Horace Miner, "Body Rituals among the Nacirema," *American Anthropologist 58* (May 1956): 504–505.

4. Carol Ember and Melvin Ember, *Cultural Anthropology* (Upper Saddle River, N.J.: Prentice Hall, 1999), 20.

5. Richard W. Brislin, *Cross-Cultural Encounters: Face-to-Face Interaction* (New York: Pergamon Press, 1981), 40–49.

6. T. Yoshitake, "A Chinese Stereotype Image of Japan and Its People," *Communication 6* (1977): 23.

7. L. Samovar, R. Porter, and N. Jain, *Understanding Intercultural Communication* (Belmont, Calif.: Wadsworth Publishing Co., 1981), 123.

8. D. W. Klopf, *Prejudice: Part 1* (San Jose, Calif.: Lansford Publishing Co., 1974), 25.

9. Brislin, *Encounters,* 48.

10. Mary Wollstonecraft, *A Vindication of the Rights of Men* (reprint, Amherst, NY: Prometheus Books, 1996), 79.

11. Cacas, "Violence against APA's on the Rise," *Asian Week* (August 4, 1995) 1, 8.

12. G. W. Allport, *The Nature of Prejudice* (Cambridge, Mass.: Addison-Wesley, 1954), 57–59.

13. Donald Klopf, *Intercultural Encounters,* (Englewood, Colo.: Morton Publishing House, 2001), 111.

Chapter 5: What Appreciating Cultural Diversity Is Not

1. James Dobson, *Family News in Focus,* Focus on the Family web site (November 1996).

2. Paul Hiebert, "Metatheology: The Step Beyond Contextualization" in *Reflection and Projection: Missiology at the Threshold of 2001,* ed. Hans Dasdorf and Klaus W. Mueller (Bad Liebenzell, Germany: Verlag der liebenzeller Mission, 1988), 384.

3. Louis Luzbetak, *The Church and Cultures* (Techny, Ill.: Divine Word Publishers, 1970), 344.

4. "The Willowbank Report: Report on a Consultation on Gospel and Culture," *Lausanne Occasional Papers,* no. 2 (Wheaton, Ill.: Lausanne Committee for World Evangelization, 1978), 28.

5. Jerry Brecheisen, *The Wesleyan Advocate* (July/August 2000): 24.

Chapter 6: How to Be Cross-Culturally Sensitive

1. Ellis Cose, "Twelve Steps Toward Racial Harmony," *Newsweek* (November 25, 1996): 54.

2. Ellen Summerfield, *Survival Kit for Multicultural Living* (Yarmouth, Maine: Intercultural Press, 1997), 106.

3. Quoted by Larry Samovar in *Understanding Intercultural Communication* (Belmont, Calif.: Wadsworth Publishing Company, 1981), 60.

4. Summerfield, *Survival Kit,* 106.

5. Quoted by Duane Elmer in *Cross-Cultural Conflict* (Downers Grove, Ill.: InterVarsity Press, 1993), 11.

6. Peter Elbow, *Embracing Contraries: Explorations in Learning and Teaching* (New York: Oxford University Press, 1986), chapter 12.

7. Ivan A. Beals, *Our Racist Legacy: Will the Church Resolve the Conflict?* vol. 9 of *Church and the World Series* (Kansas City: Cross-Cultural Publications, 1997), 169.

Chapter 7: How the Church Can Help

1. Quoted by Wayne L. Gordon and Randall Frame in *Real Hope in Chicago* (Grand Rapids: Zondervan Publishing House, 1995), 9.

2. Thomas Ehrich, "Journey," *Christianity Today* (March 4, 1996): 63.

3. Quoted by Robert M. Kaucher, "Fudge Ripple at the Rock," in *Christianity Today* (March 4, 1988): 21.

4. Quoted by Roger Bowman, "Christ Makes Men Brothers," in Black *Evangelism–Which Way From Here?* ed. R. W. Hurn (Kansas City: Nazarene Publishing House, 1974), 20:1.

5. There are many good sources for materials dealing with diversity including the following:

Intercultural Press
374 U.S. Route One
Yarmouth, ME 04096

Filmmakers Library
124 E. 40th Street, Suite 901
New York, NY 10016

University of California Extension Media Center
2176 Shattuck Avenue
Berkeley, CA 94704

Recommended videos:

Cry, the Beloved Country
Guess Who's Coming to America?
Not Without My Daughter
Pocahontas
Where the Spirit Lives